AF556223

HERMENEUTICS
AND
LANGUAGE
IN
PŪRVA MĪMĀṂSĀ

A Study in Śābara Bhāṣya

OTHMAR GÄCHTER

MOTILAL BANARSIDASS PUBLISHERS
PRIVATE LIMITED • DELHI

First Edition: Delhî, 1983
Reprinted: Delhi, 1990

ISBN: 81-208-0692-1

Also available at:
MOTILAL BANARSIDASS
Bungalow Road, Jawahar Nagar, Delhi 110 007
Chowk, Varanasi 221 001
Ashok Rajpath, Patna 800 004
24 Race Course Road, Bangalore 560 001
120 Royapettah High Road, Mylapore, Madras 600 004

PRINTED IN INDIA
BY JAINENDRA PRAKASH JAIN AT SHRI JAINENDRA PRESS, A-45 NARAINA INDUSTRIAL AREA, PHASE I, NEW DELHI 110 028 AND PUBLISHED BY NARENDRA PRAKASH JAIN FOR MOTILAL BANARSIDASS PUBLISHERS PVT. LTD., BUNGALOW ROAD, JAWAHAR NAGAR, DELHI 110007.

FOREWORD

"Heaven is happiness, and everyone seeks for happiness", says Śabara. Certainly, at all times, it lies at the root of man's effort to master life meaningfully. But is it an impelling force for life ? It is meaning that supports man, when happiness fails or is too remote from him. The desire for happiness indicates only that the source of meaning is the end.

Śabara's concern for the relevance of meaning in life is obvious in his future-oriented insight into *śruti* and *smṛti.* A critical investigation into his search for meaning does not suggest 'returning to the beginning', but involves 'turning to the future' which has left its impact on the past. Meanings appear and disappear, because man's urge to know what really is, brings into focus the validity of meaning. Meaning of the whole as present in Sacred Scriptures and accepted by people through centuries gives evidence that meanings have persisted. How do we arrive at their validity ? What is central in the search of understanding oral and written speech ? Early Pūrva Mīmāṃsā points to hermeneutics and language. Why and how, for Śabara, hermeneutics and language form the basis for such a view is critically investigated in this study.

In the introductory chapter hermeneutics and language in Pūrva Mīmāṃsā are placed within a wider context. Śabara's view of reality (chap. II) and of language (chap. III, IV) are then investigated with strict textual reference to his Bhāṣya. Thus the foundation is laid for the consequences of understanding meaning and its validity. These consequences are worked out with regard to hermeneutics as grounded in the Bhāṣya itself (chap. V, VI). Early Pūrva Mīmāṃsā shows in Śābara Bhāṣya, though not in a systematic treatment, how man participates in *satyam* (truth) through hermeneutics and language. Man's search for *satyam* is part of the vitality and authenticity of a meaningful life. It is hermeneutics and language, which provides a key in the search of meaning even today.

This book is a slightly revised form of my research submitted for the award of a Ph. D. in Philosophy at Banaras Hindu University, Varanasi. I wish to thank Prof. Dr. N. S. S. Raman for his constant readiness to supervise my research. I am greatly indebted to Dr. K. D. Tripathi, Reader of Sanskrit (Banaras Hindu University) who checked most of my English translations of the relevant Sanskrit texts, and to my friend, Dr. Jayendra Soni (Varanasi, Vienna) who checked the language of the original manuscript. Grateful acknowledgement is made to the Governments of India and Switzerland who supported the research with financial assistence under their Reciprocal Fellowship Scheme.

OTHMAR GÄCHTER

ABBREVIATIONS

AAS	Ānandāśrama Sanskrit Series 97.
FW	Frauwallner E., Mīmāṃsāsūtrabhāṣyam I, 1. 1-5.
Mī. sū.	Mīmāṃsāsūtra of Jaimini.
RV	Ṛgveda Saṃhitā.
Śā. Bhā.	Śābara Bhāṣya.
SV	Ślokavārttika of Kumārila Bhaṭṭa.
VP	Vākyapadīya of Bhartṛhari.

TABLE OF CONTENTS

Chapter I

HERMENEUTICS AND LANGUAGE IN PŪRVAMĪMĀṂSĀ : ŚĀBARA BHĀṢYA

As an outstanding compendium of sacrificial lore Śābara Bhāṣya is a source of knowledge, especially in the field of text-interpretation, which in modern terminology forms part of the discipline known as hermeneutics. The term 'hermeneutics' is complex and far reaching and inasmuch it may be described as a 'process' of understanding itself, which takes up the question of reality and language, it will be seen that it would be not inappropriate to speak of hermeneutics in Pūrva Mīmāṃsā. Insofar as the notion of hermeneutics does not stand primarily for a theory of principles of interpretations (*nyāyas*) or for a linguistic and logical method for the purposes of understanding, it may be asked whether an investigation into language as the core of hermeneutics is at all legitimate with special reference to this early Pūrva Mīmāṃsaka commentary. The problem, in other words, is that the term 'hermeneutics' is borrowed from Western philosophy and could give rise to the impression that such an investigation belongs rather to the domain of Western tradition.

Amidst the vast literature on hermeneutics and language reference may be made to H. G. GADAMER's outstanding and significant contribution *Wahrheit und Methode* (Truth and Method).[1] This classical work covers the whole range of hermeneutics and its development in the Western tradition and also shows clearly the "basic principles of a philosophical

---

1. GADAMER, H.G., *Wahrheit und Methode.* Grundzüge einer philosophischen Hermeneutik. 2. Auflage. Tübingen, 1965, English translation by W. GLEN-DOEPEL, *Truth and Method.* Second edition. London 1979. (Quoted henceforth: GADAMER, H.G., *Truth.*)

hermeneutics", as the German subtitle indicates. Thus, it may be asked whether it is possible and meaningful to elaborate a theory of hermeneutics within the philosophical context of the Indian tradition and based on the insight of Śābara Bhāṣya. Broadly speaking, the various elements of a philosophical hermeneutics have been discussed at length in the Indian tradition with great scholarship and accuracy, as for example in connection with *vāc*, *śabda*, *pratyakṣa*, *pramāṇa*, *śakti*, *buddhi*, *jñāna*, *pratyaya*, *vidyā* etc.[2] Whilst the term hermeneutics appears

---

2. cf. for example the excellent studies by:

— GARGE, D.V., Citations in Śābara-Bhāṣya, Poona, 1952 (Quoted henceforth: GARGE, D.V., *Citations*.)

— SASTRI, G., *The Philosophy of Word and Meaning*, Calcutta, 1959.

— BHATT, G.P., *Epistemology of the Bhāṭṭa School of Pūrva Mīmāṃsā*, Varanasi, 1962 (Quoted henceforth: BHATT, G.P., *Epistemology*.)

— PANDEYA, R.C., *The Problem of Meaning in Indian Philosophy*, Delhi, 1963. (Quoted henceforth: PANDEYA, R.C., *Problem*.)

— RAJA, K.K., *Indian Theories of Meaning*, Madras, 1963. (Quoted henceforth: RAJA, K.K., *Theories*.)

— BIARDEAU, M. *Théorie de la connaissance et philosophie de la Parole dans le brahmanisme classique*, Paris, 1964. (Quoted henceforth: BIARDEAU, M., *Théorie*.)

— D'SA, F.X., *Kumārila's Theorie der Worterkenntnis*, Dissertation, Wien, 1973.

— LIENHARD, S., Einige Bemerkungen über Śabdabrahman and vivarta bei Bhavabhūti, in: *Wiener Zeitschrift für die Kunde Süd-und Ostasiens und Archiv für Indische Philosophie*, 12 (1968) 216-219.

— IYER, K.A.S., *Bhartṛhari*. A study of the Vākyapadīya in the light of the Ancient Commentaries, Poona, 1969. (Quoted henceforth: IYER, K.A.S., *Bhartṛhari*.)

— DATTA, D.M., *The six Ways of Knowing*. A Critical Study of the Advaita Theory of Knowledge, Calcutta, 1972. (Quoted henceforth: DATTA, D.M., *Ways*.)

— MURTI, T.R.V., Some Comments on the Philosophy of Language in the Indian Context, in: *Journal of Indian Philosophy* (Toronto) 2 (1974) 321-331. (Quoted henceforth: MURTI, T.R.V., *Comments*.)

— MURTY, K.S., *Revelation and Reason in Advaita Vedānta*, Delhi, 1974. (Quoted henceforth: MURTY, K.S., *Revelation*.)

— DRAVID, R.R., Language, Thought and Reality, in: R.C. PANDEYA, S.R. BHATT, (eds.), *Knowledge, Culture and Value*, Delhi, 1976, pp. 447-453.

— PANIKKAR, R., *The Vedic Experience*, Mantramañjarī, London, 1977, pp. 88-112, 641-778.

only recently within Indian philosophical circles,[3] the nature of hermeneutics seems to be well expressed in Pūrva Mīmāṃsā, especially in Śābara Bhāṣya.

The notion of hermeneutics must be understood in the context of the relationship between 'language' and 'interpretation'. A few lengthy quotations by H.G. GADAMER may be very useful in this context as they point out some important aspects of modern hermeneutics :

> "I have therefore preserved the term 'hermeneutics', which the early Heidegger used, not in the sense of a methodical art, but as a theory of the real experience that thinking is. Hence I must emphasise that my analyses of play or of language are intended in a purely phenomenological sense. Play is more than the consciousness of the player; and so it is more than a subjective attitude. Language is more than the consciousness of the speaker; so it, too, is more than a subjective attitude. This is what may be described as an experience of the subject and has nothing to do with 'mythology' or 'mystification'.
>
> This fundamental methodical approach has nothing to do with any metaphysical conclusions."[4]

GADAMER further points out that according to German Romanticism "understanding and interpreting are ultimately the same thing" and with reference to Western tradition, he observes :

---

3. cf.— PANIKKAR, R., Die Begründung des hermeneutischen Pluralismus im Hinduismus, in: *Kerygma und Mythos* VI, Bd.II., Hamburg, 1964, pp. 119-136.

— CHETHIMATTAM, J.B., Scriptural Hermeneutics according to the Vedantic Bhashyakaras, in: AMALORPAVADASS, D.S., (ed.), *Research Seminar on Non-Biblical Scriptures*, Bangalore, 1974, pp. 360-365.

— PATHAK, C., Brahma-Jijñāsā as a Fundamental Hermeneutics, in: *Bharata Manisha Quarterly*, 1 (1976) No. 4. pp. 13-27.

— GREGORIOS, P., Hermeneutics in India today in the Light of the World Debate, in: *The Indian Journal of Theology*, 28 (1979) 1-14.

4. GADAMER, H.G., *Truth.*, Foreword to the second edition. p. XXIV.

"Since the romantic period we can no longer hold the view that, should there be no direct understanding, interpretative ideas are drawn on, as needed, out of a linguistic storeroom in which they are lying ready. Rather, *language is the universal medium in which understanding itself is realised. The mode of realisation of understanding is interpretation.* . . . All understanding is interpretation, and all interpretation takes place in the medium of a language which would allow the object to come into words and yet is at the same time the interpreter's own language.

Thus the hermeneutical phenomenon proves to be a special case of the general relationship between thinking and speaking, the mysterious intimacy of which is bound up with the way in which speech is contained, in a hidden way, in thinking."[5]

"Interpretation is not something pedagogical for us either, but the act of understanding itself, which is realised not just for the one for whom one is interpreting, but also for the interpreter himself in the explicitness of linguistic interpretation . . . this process is simply the concretion of the meaning itself. . . .Understanding and interpretation are indissolubly bound up with each other."[6]

Whilst the above quotations may give an insight into the nature of hermeneutics in the Western context, it is evident, however, that there is a doubt as regards the direct application of a theory of hermeneutics in the Indian context. What is also evident perhaps is the fact that the above quotations have striking parallels in Indian thought even though they may not have been elaborated upon. T.R.V. MURTI, for example, makes a very interesting comment in this regard even though he makes no explicit reference to hermeneutics. He says :

"Philosophy may be re-defined as critique of language. The problem of what we can know is closely bound up with the question of what we can say. It is only thought, as

5. GADAMER, H.G., *Truth*, pp. 350-351.
6. GADAMER, H.G., *Truth*, pp. 359-360.

expressed in words that can be understood, communicated and criticised. Language is not an accidental, dispensable garb which could be put on and put off. It grows with thought, or rather thought grows with it. In the ultimate analysis they may be identical. Bhartṛhari in his *Vākyapadīya* (I, 123) asserts this basic fact. 'There is no cognition without the operation of the word; shot through and through is cognition by the word, as it were. All knowledge is illuminated by the word.'

It is not that we have a thought, well-formed and complete, and then we seek a word to express it; or that we have a lonely word which we seek to connect with a thought. Word and thought develop together, or rather they are expressions of one deep spiritual impluse to know and to communicate. . . . It is an old and established doctrine of Bhartṛhari in India that consciousness (*Caitanya*) is identical with Speech (*Vāk*)."[7]

Whilst all the above quotations are closely related to each other in their strict concern with language, communication and understanding, however, there are important methodological differences. GADAMER, for example, lays stress on a pure phenomenological analysis together with '*Wirkungsgeschichte*' (effective history, or history as impact), whereas T.R.V. MURTI in following the transcendentalism of Bhartṛhari seems to adopt a strong metaphysical attitude. Whilst this is not the place to enter into a detailed account of the complex terms 'phenomenology' and 'metaphysics', it may be pointed out that a phenomenological approach does not necessarily imply a metaphysical standpoint or vice-versa. The phenomenologist begins with 'phenomena', whereas the metaphysician *may* begin with a notion of the absolute. GADAMER's approach, which is phenomenologically oriented, arrives at the conclusion that

7. MURTI, T.R.V., *Comments*. pp. 321-322. FN 2 Bhartṛhari, Vākyapadīya (edited by K.V. Abhyankar and V.P. Limaye), Poona, 1965, p. 12,
na so 'sti pratyayo loke yaḥ śabdānugamād ṛte
anuviddham iva jñānam sarvaṃ śabdena bhāsate.

understanding is not only, but primordially connected with the impact of history in the very act of understanding which is itself effective. In other words, the understanding of any object varies in mutual relation to the historical context in which lies the act of understanding. The philosophical context of GADAMER's approach is "Being that can be understood is language."[8] The metaphysical approach of T.R.V. MURTI who considers the Grammar School as a form of transcendentalism is evident in his conclusion that :

> "The Ultimate Ground is Transcendent, and generation of differences should be taken as a sort of emanation (*vivarta*) which does not affect the Ultimate Cause. Bhartṛhari sees the entire world as a non-transforming emanation of the Non-Dual Brahman, the *WORD*. . . .Why should the non-dual Brahman, in which the distinction of Word and Meaning has not emerged, be identified with the Essence of Speech (*Śabda-Tattva*) ? Because it is the Causal Ground of the Word and because it is so realised in the order of our discovery, through analysis of the Word-Symbolism."[9]

Consequently, whilst noticing the striking parallels of a hermeneutical concern in both traditions, one has to be cautious in adopting the presumptions both of a phenomenological, historical approach on the one hand and a transcendental or metaphysical approach on the other.

Hermeneutics with reference to Śābara Bhāṣya must be based on the insight of this early Pūrva Mīmāṃsaka philosopher.

---

8. GADAMER'S concern, moreover, does not avoid ontological questions as is evident from Part III of *Truth and Method* (pp. 342-447) which is entitled "The Ontological Shift of Hermeneutics guided by Language", of which the last chapter is called "Language as Horizon of a Hermeneutic Ontology".

9. MUTRI, T.R.V., *Comments* p. 331. It seems that T.R.V. MURTI has overlooked GADAMER's ontological contribution when he says "Linguistic speculations in the West do not reach out beyond the phenomenological sphere — the realm of ideational, linguistic discourse. Ontological questions are not considered, and are even studiously avoided" (*Comments*, p. 330).

Thus our approach is obviously connected with the realism of Śabara. It is from this viewpoint that language, communication, interpretation and understanding are brought into focus. The guiding idea of our analysis is not to arrive at a 'special' or 'regional hermeneutics'. As K. LEHMANN points out aptly with reference to the interpretation of Rabbinical Scripture, the task of regional hermeneutics is to ensure against particular mistakes and to provide the relevant application or normative repetition of a tradition.

> "This hermeneutics has a concrete way of understanding in mind, for which it draws up a canon of rules with which to approach the tradition, especially the texts. ... But such hermeneutics were simply the sum of concrete guides to right understanding derived from experience, and were mostly applied to fixed systems, of acknowledgedly authoritative character, which aimed at the right practice. They aimed at an elaborate 'art' or technique of understanding, which is far from what is meant by a 'theory of understanding' such as constitutes the modern concept of hermeneutics."[10]

No matter how much a regional hermeneutics can be discovered in Pūrva Mīmāṃsā, the fact is that the problems of regional hermeneutics are already problems of understanding itself. Thus this study on hermeneutics in Pūrva Mīmāṃsā rather attempts to answer the question "What does it really mean to understand, whereby the problem centres around the acquisition of knowledge as Śabara presents it. Such an acquisition of knowledge as it is focused in the act of understanding reality may be said to be the task of hermeneutics. To unfold this task and to show how it can be achieved the study is based on the view of reality and language as expressed in Śābara Bhāṣya.

Reality, according to Śabara's view, encompasses everything that was, is and can be, and this single reality is

10. LEHMANN, K., Hermeneutics, in: RAHNER, K., ERNST, C., SMYTH, K. (eds.), *Sacramentum Mundi*. An Encyclopedia of Theology. Vol. 3. (reprint) Bangalore 1975, pp. 23-27, p. 23, col. 2.

conveniently characterised by the two dimensions of the *dṛṣṭa* (visible) and the *adṛṣṭa* (invisible), which are arrived at on the basis of *pratyakṣa* and *śabda*.[11] The distinction of reality into the two dimensions of the *dṛṣṭa* and the *adṛṣṭa* lays bare the whole problem of language and thereby indicates the nature, significance and relevance of language for hermeneutics. The nature of language according to Śābara Bhāṣya involves the consideration of the characteristics of *śabda*, whilst the function of meaningful and valid speech is explained with reference to *śabda* and the Vedas. It is in this context that the connection of hermeneutics and language in Pūrva Mīmāṃsā gains crucial importance. The fundamental question is the validity of cognition and especially the possibility of knowledge in view of *śabda* as a *pramāṇa*. This is the point at which Śabara's main concern with *dharma* indicates, especially, the nature of hermeneutics (*dharmāya jijñāsā dharmajijñāsā. sā hi tasya jñātum icchā* (Śā. Bhā. 1. 1. 1)). This concern may be said to be a hermeneutical one, as it shows Śabara's fundamental urge and wish to know what really *is*. Thus the hermeneutical concern centres around the problem of proper understanding in hermeneutical awareness. How hermeneutical awareness can be achieved is considered in connection with the nature, significance and relevance of language. Hermeneutics and language in Śābara Bhāṣya are thus indissolubly bound up with each other.

The Bhāṣya attributed to Śabara is the oldest available commentary on the Mīmāṃsā Sūtra of Jaimini. It is the earliest available work in the systematised form of Pūrva Mīmāṃsā. In the words of F. ZANGENBERG :

> "Besides the collection of Sūtras which is assigned to Jaimini there is one commentary on it that is extant, as the earliest work in the Mīmāṃsā, namely the Bhāṣya of Śabara,

---

11. The distinction of the *dṛṣṭa* and the *adṛṣṭa* with reference to Śābara Bhāṣya seems to have been fully elaborated first by M. BIARDEAU in her outstanding work *Théorie de la connaissance et philosophie de la parole dans le brahmanisme classique*, Paris, 1964. The second chapter of Part I is entitled: "*Perception et Parole*: *Connaissance du visible et de l'invisble*" (Perception and Speech: cognition of the visible and the invisible) p. 65; cf. Mīmāṃsā pp. 68-99.

which could belong to the 5th century A.D. All the Mīmāṃsā works preceding the Bhāṣya which are acknowledged in numerous accounts of subsequent literature, have therefore to be considered as lost."[12]

Whilst the date of Jaimini's Mīmāṃsā Sūtras is usually placed between 400-200 B.C., D.V. GARGE's considerations lead to the conclusion "that the extant JS falls into the earlier part of the Śrautasūtra period, i.e. circa 500 B.C."[13] Although Śābara Bhāṣya has sometimes been placed as early as 100 B.C.[14], GARGE's investigation indicates "the second century A.D. as the earliest date to which Śabara can be assigned; the later limit being the 5th century A.D."[15], which is accepted by M. BIARDEAU, F. ZANGENBERG and E. FRAUWALLNER. Further, the latter two have furnished new evidence in favour of the fact that Śābara Bhāṣya belongs to the 5th century A.D. ZANGENBERG points out with reference to the epistemologies of the Vṛttikāra quoted in Śābara Bhāṣya, of the Sāṅkhya author Vṛṣagaṇa (probably 4th century A.D.) and of Vasubandhu (about 400-480 A.D.) that the Vṛttikāra and Śabara have to be placed in the 5th century A.D.[16] FRAUWALLNER on the other hand establishes the date of Śābara Bhāṣya as

---

12. ZANGENBERG, F., Śabaraḥ und seine philosophischen Quellen, in *Wiener Zeitschrift für die Kunde Süd-und Ostasiens und Archiv für Indische Philosophie* 6 (1962) 60-77, p. 60. (Quoted henceforth: ZANGENBERG, F., *Śabaraḥ*.)

For a discussion of the pre-Śabara Mīmāṃsakas cf. MISRA, Umesha, Critical Bibliography of Mīmāṃsā pp. 1-16 (Quoted henceforth: MISRA, U., *Bibliography*.), which is published as appendix in JHA, Ganganatha, *Pūrva-Mīmāṃsā in its Sources*, Varanasi, 1942, and GARGE, D. V., *Citations*, pp. 5-8.

13. GARGE, D.V., *Citations*, p. 17. For a discussion of the age of Jaimini cf. pp. 13-17 and also MISRA, U., *Bibliography*, p. 13.

14. MURTY, K.S., *Revelation*, p. 195. That Śābara Bhāṣya has not to be placed later than 100 B.C. has already been suggested by DEVASTHALI, G.V., On the probable date of Śabarasvāmin, *Silver Jubilee Volume*, Bhandarkar Institute 1917-42, Poona, p. 95. GARGE discusses the age of Śabara in some detail, Cf. GARGE, D.V., Citations pp. 23-26.

15. GARGE, D.V., *Citations*, p. 26.

16. ZANGENBERG, F., *Śabaraḥ*, pp. 60-70.

belonging to the 5th century A.D. in the following way : The Pramāṇasamuccaya of the Buddhist Dignāga quotes the name of Vṛttikāra who most probably is Bhavadāsa who belongs to the first half of the 5th century A.D. Śabara also quotes the name of Vṛttikāra who must be considered with reference to the Vādavidhi of Vasubandhu and who consequently must be said to belong to the second half of the 5th century A.D. Thus according to FRAUWALLNER the Vṛttikāra of Dignāga and the Vṛttikāra of Śabara must be distinguished as different authors and consequently the date of the Bhāṣya of Śabara cannot be placed before the 5th century A.D.[17]

Moreover ZANGENBERG and FRAUWALLNER have drawn attention to the extreme difficulty in attempting to trace the philosophical influences and sources of Śabara's views,

> "because the earlier literature is lost and the casual remarks of the authors after Śabara cannot be taken into account, because they are not in agreement and an answer cannot be derived from them."[18]

Further Śabara often quotes views and passages from the Vedas, and the *smṛti* without direct reference to their sources. GARGE points out that little effort has been made in tracing the original sources of the citations in Śābara Bhāṣya which would assist in a better understanding of the work, which has influenced later philosophical development.[19] However, the present investigation takes as Śabara's own words whatever seems to give support to his view as a whole.

Besides FRAUWALLNER has interestingly dealt with the problem of what is considered to have been later insertions in

---

17. FRAUWALLNER, E., *Materialien zur ältesten Erkenntnislehre der Karmamīmāṃsā*, Wien, 1968 (Quoted henceforth: FRAUWALLNER, E., *Materialien.*), especially "Die Polemik gegen die Mīmāṃsā in Dignāga's Pramāṇasamuccayaḥ" 62-103, pp. 95-103 and also "Der Vṛttikāraḥ" pp. 107-115.

18. ZANGENBERG, F., *Śabaraḥ*, p. 61. cf. also GARGE, D.V., *Citations*, pp. 28-29.

19. GARGE, D.V., *Citations*, p. 27, 28-32.

the original Bhāṣya of Śabara. On the basis of the linguistic style, the arrangement of ideas and on the basis of what can be considered to be views prevalent at the time of Śabara, FRAUWALLNER suggests that there are some sūtra portions in the Bhāṣya which are not original. For example the portion of Śābara Bhāṣya 1. 1. 6-23 mentions especially the *nityatva* character of *śabda* which FRAUWALLNER translates as "die Ewigkeit des Tones" (eternity of sound). In the context of the Bhāṣya as a whole and especially Śā. Bhā. 1. 1. 15 and 1. 1. 24 FRAUWALLNER feels that this section is inconsistent. Further, the notion of "eternity of sound" was not prevalent at the time of Śabara and became dominant only later, especially at the time of Kumārila Bhaṭṭa who in his commentary on Śābara Bhāṣya deals with this section.[20] FRAUWALLNER's suggestion is no doubt interesting and could perhaps be proved on the basis of historical philological evidences. However, the notion of *nityatva* does not seem to be out of the context of Śābara Bhāṣya. The notion of *nityatva* may be more correctly rendered as 'permanence' rather than 'eternity' which would be consistent with Śabara's view as a whole. Further the textual unit which is generally accepted today as being the authentic Bhāṣya includes the sūtras which FRAUWALLNER considers to be a later insertion. Moreover, this section supports Śabara's entire view of language and reality and deserves full consideration.

---

20. FRAUWALLNER, Erich, Mīmāṃsāsūtram I, 1, 6-23, in: *Wiener Zeitschrift für die Kunde Süd—und Ostasiens und Archiv für Indische Philosophie*, 5 (1961) 113-124 (Quoted henceforth: FRAUWALLNER, E., *Mīmāṃsāsūtram*, I, 1. 6-23.).

FRAUWALLNER, E., Das Eindringen der Sprachtheorie in die Indischen philosophischen Systeme. *Indologentagung* 1959. *Verhandlungen der Indol. Arbeitstagung in Essen-Bredeny*, Göttingen 1960, 239-243.

FRAUWALLNER, E., Sprachtheorie und Philosophie im Mahābhāṣyam des Patañjali, in: *Wiener Zeitschrift für die Kunde Süd- und Ostasiens und Archiv für Indische Philosophie*, 4 (1960) 92-118, especially pp. 111-118.

Chapter II

ŚABARA'S VIEW OF REALITY

In order to reach *dharma*[1] man has to live within his field of experience which according to Śābara Bhāṣya is intrinsically related to reality as a whole. In fact, Śabara's main concern, the realization of *dharma*, depends largely on the understanding of reality. Thus *dharma* is considered and realized in the two dimensions of reality : the visible (*dṛṣṭa*) and the invisible (*adṛṣṭa*). Śabara, in general, takes for granted as visible reality, whatever is *pratyakṣa* and *vyapadeśya*, i.e., whatever can be perceived and

---

1. Mī. sū. 1.1.2: "*Dharma* is the object that is indicated by the Vedic injunctions". (see text p. 125)

Śā. Bhā. 1.1.2: "That which is indicated by the (Vedic injunctions) is the object (*dharma*) which brings man to the highest good. This is our thesis". (see text p. 125)

"*Dharma* according to the context is the assemblage of the Vedic rites prescribed in order to reach 'heaven' after death and welfare in this world or the conduct that is considered to be meritorious because it is recommended by the orthodox tradition and it assures good rebirths. Accepting the latter *dharma* contains still the Vedic rites but comprehends as well the conduct in a more proper ethical view. It is also a 'quality' of a thing or a being and in Buddhism the thing itself". (BIARDEAU, M., *Théorie*, p. 466.)

Ganganatha JHA emphasizes that *dharma* is used in the sense of what should be done, i.e., duty, and 'what is moral'. cf. JHA, G., *Pūrva-Mīmāṃsā in its Sources*, Varanası, 1964, pp. 152-154 (Quoted heneforth: JHA, G., *Pūrva-Mīmāṃsā.*) and also his translation: *Śābara-Bhāṣya*, 3 vols, Gaekwad's Oriental Series No. 66.70.73, Baroda (Quoted henceforth: JHA, G., *Śābara-Bhāṣya*). (especially with reference to Śā. Bhā. 1.1.2 in vol. I, pp. 6-7 and the introduction in vol. III. p. VIII.).

R.C. PANDEYA comments upon Mī. Sū. 1.1.2: "The *Mīmāṃsā Sūtras* set out to examine the duty of human beings (*dharma*). Duty was defined as imperative. That which gives oneself some urge is called duty" (*Problem*, p. 13).

named/expressed.[2] If an object is open to sense perception, it belongs to the visible dimension of reality (*dṛṣṭa*), e.g. cow, fire, the various ingredients of a sacrifice, etc. Everything else which is not the outcome of mere imagination belongs to the invisible dimension (*adṛṣṭa*). As for the invisible reality, he points, for example, to *svarga* (heaven), *devatā* (deity) and *apūrva* (what previously did not exist, what is new). The core of both (*dṛṣṭa* and *adṛṣṭa*), as far as it is cognized, is *arthālambanaḥ* (has a real object as support)[3], though as we shall see, in different ways. Here the pivotal significance of *śabda*[4] becomes very obvious, because according to Śābara Bhāṣya *śabda* finally forms and structures the whole experience and whatever is related to it. It is the key to all investigations into hermeneutics and language and is directly related to human experience.

T.R.V. MURTI points out that "The Mīmāṃsā which is ostensibly concerned with dharma—performance of the sacrifices and rites — finds that the investigation of dharma involves metaphysical and epistemological issues about the self, nature of karma etc. It is committed to a form of Realism". (*The Central Philosophy of Buddhism*, London 1974, pp. 29-30).

For recent discussion on *dharma* see:

— MISRA, R.S., The Meaning of Dharma, in: *Studies in Philosophy and Religion*, Varanasi, 1971, pp. 118-140.

— MANICKAM, T.M., Manu's Vision of the Hindu Dharma, in: *Journal of Dharma*, 1 (1975) 101-117.

— KUPPUSWAMY, B., A Modern Review of Hindu Dharma, in: *Journal of Dharma*, 1 (1975) 118-136.

2. cf. the discussion on *buddhi* and *artha* in the context of *pratyakṣa* in Śā. Bhā. 1.1.5 (see text p. 125)

3. Śā. Bhā. 1.1.5 (FW 30, 12-13): *arthālambanaḥ pratyayaḥ* "Cognition has its substratum in the object" (G. JHA).

M. BIARDEAU comments : " 'La connaissance a l'object réel pour support', et non *pratyakṣaḥ*, 'la perception'. *Pratyaya* est ici le synonyme de *jñāna* et désigne n'importe quelle connaissance" (*Théorie*, p. 76). ('The knowledge has the real object as support' and not *pratyakṣa*, 'the perception'. *Pratyaya* is here the synonym of *jñāna* and denotes any kind of knowledge.)

4. *śabda*: sound, noise, word, speech, etc. cf. the multidimensional meaning of *śabda* below pp. 39-41.

1. *The dṛṣṭa or the Visible*

> "In worldly affairs action is determined by things; it is not indicated by words. One acts in accordance with the (state of) things and not in accordance with words. But in Vedic action the thing is known only through the word. Hence actions should be done in accordance with words."[5]

In the investigation of language Śabara's comment demonstrates clearly the importance of things and the relevance of words to man's experience.

Man's experience is related to the state of things (*artha*). *Artha* has a multidimensional meaning and in Śābara Bhāṣya it usually indicates 'object, thing'[6], 'aim, purpose'[7], 'sense, meaning'.[8] In spite of this wide range of meanings there seems to be often an emphasis on *artha* as an object, i.e., on things required for sacrifice. For Śabara things and objects must be capable of being clearly indicated or described. In fact "the external object has a form and it is directly perceived as connected with external space."[9] This suggests that there is no factual observation of things or objects without form (*ākāra*). In fact, "when we directly perceive an object, we perceive it with a form."[10] The whole emphasis is laid on the direct perception of a real object that is accessible to sense perception by its form and structure (*ākāra*).

Ākāra connotes "form, figure, shape, stature, appearance."[11] It is the "direct object of perception" and the pregnant aspect of the object that is noticed and makes it known". Besides "*ākāra* is also the lay-out in the external space". It is objective.[12]

---

5. Śā. Bhā. 6.8.27 (see text p. 134).
6. Śā. Bhā. 1.1.5 (see text p. 125).
7. Śā. Bhā. 6.1.2 (see text p. 134).
8. Śā. Bhā. 9.1.9 (see text p. 134).
9. cf. Serial no. 6: Śā. Bhā. 1.1.5 (FW 28, 17-19).
10. cf. Serial no. 6: Śā. Bhā. 1.1.8 (FW 30, 12-13).
11. MONIER-WILLIAMS, *A Sanskrit-English Dictionary*, Delhi, 1974, p. 127, col. 2; cf. *ā-kṛ* to bring near or towards (quoted henceforth: MONIER-WILLIAMS, *Dictionary*.)
12. "La notion qui fait le nerf de la démonstration est celle d'*ākāra*, de 'forme structurée'; ... L'*ākāra* est l'object direct de la perception...Il

Hence the object is real and accessible to sense perception (*pratyakṣa*). There is a visible dimension which is neither inferred nor has its own existence apart from the object.[13] The object gives support to cognition.[14] Ideas might be inferred thereof, but they are only valid as a result of this objective source and these ideas do not exist in themselves apart from the object. If ideas are only the products of a human mind, then they are unreliable. Neither sense perception nor a human source as such are a guarantee for a reliable source of knowing a thing, if it is not within the objective realm of sense perception which has the support of the real object. It is, therefore, the object in the realm of visibility that can become experiential, factual knowledge.

Although the objects are not eternal, i.e., they have a concrete beginning, continuation and an end, as they come into existence and perish,[15] they are nonetheless in contact with *ātman* (self) which is equated with *nitya* (permanent).[16] The object forms an entity, which is characterized by stability, as we cannot perceive any change within it. It is worth emphasizing

---

est l'aspect prégnant de l'objet, ce que l'on remarque et qui le fait reconnaître. L'*ākāra* est aussi d'emblée situé dans l'espace externe". (BIARDEAU, M., *Théorie*, p. 75)

13. cf. Serial No. 2: Śā. Bhā. 1.1.5

14. cf. Serial No. 6: Śā. Bhā. 1.1.5 (FW 30, 12-13)

15. cf. Śā. Bhā. 2.1.3: "When words serve their object while they are pronounced, one apprehends a form which, having come into existence once, continues to exist for some time, i.e., the object does not perish as soon as it comes into existence like an act and these words are names; they express substances and qualities. (See text p. 134).

16. Śābara Bhāṣya refers in this context to the Bṛhadāraṇyakopaniṣad 3, 2, 25; 4, 3, 9; 4, 5, 13, 15, 23; 5, 4, 11 and the Śatapatha Brāhmaṇa Mādhyandina 14, 7, 3, 15. The Bhāsya concludes with the latter. "'This *ātman*, verily, is imperishable and of indestructible nature; but there is contact with the elements (perishable things)". [Śā. Bhā. 1.1.5 (FW 60, 21-22), see text p. 125].

cf. also Śā. Bhā. 1.1.5 (FW 58, 23-24): "Certainly he knows from evanescent (activities) the enduring" see text p. 125).

G. JHA remarks in this context: "Or, on the basis of the evanescent activities one comes to cognise the enduring Self" (Śābara-Bhāṣya, vol. I., p. 30).

that "the only means of knowing objects is to realize that 'everything *is* as it is cognised to be.' "[17] Objects, due to their shape and form, support knowledge insofar as they are cognised. The fact of recognition points to *ātman*, as this notion of recognition appears only in the inner self.[18] The self that is not perishable, but enduring, must be something distinct from the cognition which is evanescent.[19] *Ātman* itself cannot be shown in its structure, but man is aware of the *ātman* because of self-luminosity.[20] In fact, it is not apart from the one who perceives himself.[21]

It is important to note that *ātman* is alive with *puruṣa* (man) because the human body is the link between *ātman* and *artha* through perception. As there is no human cognition without *ātman and* the *object*, knowledge must be accessible to man in order to be real. It arises when *artha* (object) and *puruṣa* (man) are in inseparable unity with *ātman.* Thus two dimensions of reality are focused in man. One dimension includes what is *nitya* (permanent) and *apauruṣeya* (not made by a human or divine agent) and other includes what is a stable object.[22] Entities which are not permanent, though lasting (i.e. not momentary), being *dṛṣṭa*, come into contact with the *adṛṣṭa*,

---

17. Śā. Bhā. 1.1.5 (see text p. 125).
18. Śā. Bhā. 1.1.5 (see text p. 126).
19. Śā. Bhā. 1.1.5: "After it has been declared 'this, verily, is the *ātman*', it is said 'It is imperishable, for it is not to be destroyed'. Further 'this *ātman*, verily, is imperishable and of indestructible nature'. Cognition on the other hand is evanescent. Hence we conclude that it is different from (that which is) evanescent." (see text p. 126).
20. Śā. Bhā. 1.1.5: "Because of the statement 'there is self-luminosity'. There is also a Brāhmaṇa-text: 'In that state the person becomes self-illuminated' (i.e., self-luminous)." (see text p. 126).
21. cf. Serial No. 16 Śā. Bhā. 1.1.5. (FW 58, 23-24). "Thus all perceive (their) *ātman* through their own *ātman*, even though they are not perceived by other people. In support of this there is the Brāhmaṇa-text 'when speech ceases, what light does the person have? - He has the light of the *ātman* (*ātmajyotiḥ*), O king so did he say." (see text p. 126).
22. cf. Serial No. 15.16.21. Śā. Bhā. 1.1.5: "We perceive the *ātman* through desire. ... If, on the other hand, there is a cogniser apart from the cognition, who is permanent, then the same (person) who perceived (something) on one day, desires (it) on the other day. The desire would be impossible otherwise." (see text p. 126). cf. also Serial No. 19.

whose features are permanent, and with the *apauruṣeya*. But the *dṛṣṭa* and the *adṛṣṭa* are not merged into one another, though they form one reality. Both these dimensions belong to the same reality and are in spite of their different features inseparable from one another with regard to knowledge. Man is directed to reality in both its visible and invisible dimensions. Both dimensions are accessible only through man, for whose benefit reality exists.

Actually there is a mutual support between *ātman* and *artha* (object), insofar as Śābara Bhāṣya throws light on the problem of cognition and perception. The body, which is *artha* as well, does not exist without the self as seat of pleasure and pain. Thus *artha* seems to be supported by *ātman*. However, the *ātman* is regarded as distinct from cognition on the ground of the self-realization of the one who is involved.[23]

Further the *ātman* is not realized without *artha*, i.e. without the body, without bodily existence, but *ātman* is not bound to it. However, this body-*ātman* relation becomes only obvious through inference, which finally rests on the perception of feelings, breathing and desire.[24] So *ātman* as the cogniser is self-cognised. *Ātman* cannot be perceived by anyone other than oneself, but one can make the other aware of one's own *ātman*.[25] *Ātman* is not something that is yet to come, but exists even

---

23. Śā. Bhā. 1.1.5 (see text p. 126). G. JHA sums up the passage, when, in a very free translation, he points out: "Thus on the ground of this self-realization, it is concluded that there is a person (self) distinct from cognition" (*Śābara-Bhāṣya*, vol. I., p. 30).

24. This can be seen from the link in the explanation of the sacrificer who goes straight to heaven (with reference to pleasure and pain) and *ātman* (with reference to cognition, desire and memory).

Śā. Bhā. 1.1.5: "On account of the connection with the body because of the sacrificial implements the one to whom the body belongs is also spoken of as 'equipped with sacrificial implements'. (The opponent) says: Who is this other? We do not perceive him.—(Answer) We obtain it through breathing etc. ... Breathing etc. are no properties of the body. ... Further, pleasure etc. (pain and such feelings) are perceived by (the person) himself. ... Hence, on account of the properties being different from those of the body the one who is equipped with sacrificial implements is other than the body". (see text p. 126).

25. cf. Serial No. 21

when it is not known. But *artha* (object) is really present (not non-existent), if it can be apprehended by sense perception. Both *ātman* and *artha* are presupposed in man. *Ātman* is given as existing permanently, while *artha* has limitation. Knowledge, therefore, is confined to the interaction between the *dṛṣṭa* and the *adṛṣṭa*.

There is change in the world that cannot be presupposed in spite of the permanence of *ātman* and in spite of the limitations of the object. Man is aware of change by perceiving similarity and difference of objects. The object is not permanent and *ātman* is not affected by the thing which undergoes change. This change of the object, however, does not characterize the physical reality which is ever in process. The formation of world is still considered to be within a whole which is stable—without creation (*sṛṣṭi*) and dissolution (*pralaya*), as Kumārila Bhaṭṭa has formulated it.[26]

The only access to the visible dimension of reality is based on sense perception. Although sense perception is itself within the visible dimension, reality is not limited by it or reduced to it. The invisible is supported by the visible and vice versa; both the visible and the invisible are dimensions of reality wherein they are related to things which can be perceived. Things of the world are related to man directly and talking of things perceived independently of man is to make reality meaningless. Things are given within the whole and do not carry any meaning and being in themselves set apart from the whole, which includes man. This does not suggest that meaning is added to things in an attitude of mere name giving by men, but that things are meaningful for men in their concrete, real structure for human experience without being bound only to a human sphere of reality. The realm of visibility (*dṛṣṭa*) of human experience shows clearly that it is only one aspect of reality, which does not indicate another reality beyond the one perceived, but is does point to another aspect of reality the *adṛṣṭa* (invisible).

26. cf. Kumārila's Ślokavārttikam, Sambandhākṣepaparihāraḥ, vv. 42-117, esp. 47, 67.68.

2. *The adṛṣṭa or the Invisible*

Actions according to Śabara have various and different results depending upon the object which is in the realm of visibility. If the object is in connection with a Vedic sacrifice, the result must not belong to the realm of visibility. Śābara Bhāṣya II,2,25-26 may serve as an illustration to show how far the object gives support to the visible and the invisible.

Śabara's opponent explains that in order to obtain 'sense-efficiency' through a sacrificial act, grain is used. Can grain produce an invisible result ?—In fact agricultural operations do not produce an invisible result. And he continues :

> " 'Besides there is no invisible (result) from an agricultural operation; the *homa* as it is similar to it, also is not likely to bring about an invisible (result). It is likely to bring about only (grains of) rice, because of its similarity to an agricultural operation, no sense-efficiency'.
>
> 'It is, therefore, with regard to such matters not (true) that the invisible is attained (proved) by the visible'.
>
> 'How is it then that the result follows from a *homa ?*'
>
> 'Our answer is that one knows from *śabda* that there will be a result. Whereof *śabda* speaks, thereof a result follows. Hence it is justifiable (to maintain this position)....
>
> Hence the correct view is that the result (sense-efficiency) follows from the *homa* and it is unreasonable to say the result follows from (the material) *dadhi*.' "[27]

There is no doubt that according to Śabara in referring to Vedic acts "the thing is known only through the word. Hence actions should be done in accordance with words."[28] Nevertheless Śabara objects to the explanation mentioned above by quoting the Vṛttikāra :

> " 'The material as resting in the *homa* brings about the result, as the officer of the king, who subsists on the king,

---

27. Śā. Bhā. 2.2.25 (see text p. 134).

28. See Serial No. 5: Śā. Bhā. 6.8.27 and also Serial No. 27. Cf. below chapter IV. Śabara's View of Language: *Śabda* in Vedic and non-Vedic Speech, pp. 70-84.

performs the works of the king. Thus the result follows from *dadhi*. One who desires sense-efficiency should bring about sense-efficiency by means of *dadhi*'. ... 'It is because of the indication of what has to be done that the result follows from the accomplishment with *dadhi*. ... Hence the result follows from the (use of the) *dadhi*'. ... or 'There will be the result from *dadhi* in connection with the *homa*'."[29]

Śabara gives a great significance to *śabda* (word, Veda) and, therefore, he does *not* abandon the object (*dravya*) at all. The grains or *dadhi* do not change the *ākāra*, whether they are used for a visible or invisible result, within or without a sacrificial act. In our context *dadhi* supports reality in both its aspects of visibility and invisibility.

The visible and the invisible dimensions of reality are connected here by a specific object (*dadhi*), although the visible means, the material, must not be stated explicitly (for example "*agnihotraṃ juhuyāt svargakāmaḥ*", i.e., we have only a result, heaven, mentioned along with an act).[30] However, the object within the visible dimension of reality, cannot be abandoned from the invisible dimension of reality although we do know about the latter only by inference. This inference is wrong, if our perception is wrong. Hence in our example the object is abandoned only by a wrong perception of *dadhi* and only because of such an error the object would not lead to an invisible result within an otherwise correct sacrificial procedure. It must be noted that the object can be used only in the visible reality to give support to the existence of what cannot be perceived by sense perception, namely the invisible; it will have to be used correctly in a sacrificial act. If the object is used for a result in the visible dimension of reality (as in the case of agricultural acts), the object is not thereby linked with the invisible dimension of reality.

According to Śabara the invisible dimension is indicated by *śabda* (word, Veda). Yet his explanation shows, to a certain

---

29. Śa. Bha. 2.2.26 (see text p. 134).
30. Śā. Bhā. 2.2.26 (see text p. 134).

extent, how by a correct use of an object the invisible dimension of reality is supported by the visible one,[31] but not vice versa. This seems to be often the case with regard to the invisible dimension, which is presented, for example, by *svarga, devatā, apūrva,* although their presentation and presence are different from one another.

(i) *Svarga*

The use of '*svarga*' (heaven) occurs in ancient *smṛti* texts, in the Vedas and also in the popular use of the term in the time of Śābara Bhāṣya.[32] We come across it in assertions like

> " 'Fine silken clothes are heaven', 'Sandal paste is heaven', 'Sixteen-year old girls are heaven'. In fact, anything that is pleasant is spoken of as heaven. Therefore we are of the opinion that it follows from the common function that heaven is a pleasure-giving substance...
>
> The word heaven is well known in common usage with regard to a particular region, where neither heat nor cold (exists), neither hunger nor thirst.
>
> There is neither lack of fondness nor any tiredness. Who has led a virtuous life goes there after death, but nobody else."[33]

The use of '*svarga*' in such statements as "fine silken clothes are heaven" could make it a clear-cut object which is not beyond sense perception nor beyond one's physical reach. In such a case *svarga* would be an accomplished entity. Although *svarga* is illuminated by statements based on sense-experience, these statements serve only as a "pointer" to the actual *svarga.*

In fact Śabara vehemently opposes all descriptive statements of *svarga*, because, as he says, human experience does not

---

31. The visible points to the invisible in other ways as well as, for example, in the relation between the body and the *ātman*, and in human perception of cognition. (cf. above pp. 15-18).

32. cf. above pp. 9-10.

33. Śā. Bhā. 6.1.1 (see text p. 135).

provide us with any direct support of *svarga.*[34] *Svarga* cannot be established or recognised on the basis of the contact between senses and the object of sense-experience, which forms the visible dimension of reality. This view according to Śabara, does neither prove the non-existence of *svarga* nor deny man's desire for it. Heaven is something to be "enjoyed" and all descriptions of it fall short of actually grasping it. Statements are nothing but those made within an anthropomorphical framework which breaks down, as soon as one realizes that *svarga* is not to be experienced by man on the basis of sense perception. Although it is something that can and has to be reached and obtained, it is not available as some specified object at the moment when one desires it. Heaven, according to Śabara, has to be realized (*sādhya*) and this is made possible only by being involved in sacrificial acts.

This link between man, sacrifice and heaven is essential, because heaven *and* sacrifice cannot be made exclusive of each other and these are meaningless without reference to the man performing the sacrifice with the view to achieving heaven.[35] An act in the visible dimension, namely sacrifice, leads to the invisible dimension, namely heaven (*svarga*). Thus, *svarga* is only possible by the correct performance of the sacrificial act. Further, *svarga* has its support only in *ātman* which is not at all affected by man's physical death. Although it is only the *ātman* that enjoys *svarga*, nonetheless man (as the physical

---

34. Śā. Bhā. 6.1.1. "There is no *pramāṇa* (in support of the statement that) there are such men with powers (*siddha*) and that they have described (the heavenly region) after having seen it. Hence there is indeed no such region. ... Since there is no human activity in relation to any such region the *svargaśabda*, therefore, cannot be considered as expressive of it" (see text p. 135).

35. Śā. Bhā. 6.1.2: "Thus in order not to consider (the sacrifice) as useless the possibility of (bringing about) heaven is (must) to be understood. And as the activity of man is qualified by the sacrifice, the sacrifice should be the means to it. Thus it is well said that the 'sacrifice' is the subordinate factor and 'heaven' the principal factor" (see text p. 135).

Śā. Bhā. 6.1.3: "An activity is undertaken with a view to some desired object. For one who desires heaven, *heaven* is the desired object. The distinct reference of 'one who desires heaven is only for the purpose of indicating *that* particular activity. This is flawless". (see text p. 135).

embodiment of the *ātman*) makes an effort with the view of obtaining happiness,[36] which depends on his performance of the sacrifice.

Svarga arising from man's sacrifice cannot be grasped as a substance, as it never fully reveals itself in its pure state to sense perception. "Heaven is *happiness*, and everyone seeks for happiness..." a word that cannot be restricted to anything particuiar.[37] "Heaven is the result of an action whose result is not specified."[38] All categories are inadequate and break down, when they are applied to the realm of invisibility. For Śabara there is, however, neither an indication nor a justification for assuming a reality which is beyond man's reach. The two dimensions of reality for Śabara are *dṛṣṭa* and *adṛṣṭa* and they cannot be considered as two independent realities. We can only say that *svarga*, which belongs to the invisible dimension of reality, is real and that we cannot describe its existence by means of definitions. Although it is invisible, it is within man's reach through his effort in sacrifice. *Svarga* does not make any specific distinction among men. Anyone can either perform or be involved in a sacrifice. Even if the result is not specifically mentioned in the context of a particular sacrificial act, the result will still be *svarga* (heaven/happiness), because "this (result) would be 'heaven', as that is equally desirable for all. In fact, all men desire heaven."[39]

(ii) *Devatā*

"Deities are those who are *Sūktabhāk* (to whom hymns are addressed) and *Havirbhāk* (recipients of offerings)."[40] The *devatā* that is usually mentioned in Śābara Bhāṣya is in connection with the performance of sacrifices and thereby belongs

---

36. Śā, Bhā. 6.1.2: "In this case, however, *svargaśabda* verily denotes happiness. If it means happiness, then the sacrifice is the subordinate factor and happiness the principal factor.—Why so—Because man's effort is for that purpose; for man makes an effort in order to obtain happiness" (see text p. 135).
37. Śā. Bhā. 4.3.15 (see text p. 135).
38. Śā. Bhā. 4.3.16 (see text p. 136).
39. Śā. Bhā. 4.3.15 (see text p. 136).
40. Śā. Bhā. 10.4.23 (see text p. 136).

to the reality in which we live. In the context of the two dimensions of reality it becomes pertinent to ask whether a *devatā* is present as *dṛṣṭa* or *adṛṣṭa*.

Śabara rejects strongly any human experience of a *devatā*. He 'demythologises' those statements made in the *smṛti* texts and known by custom and indicative texts, which pretend to speak about a certain behaviour and/or qualities of the *devatā*. e.g. eating habits, rewarding people with wealth and strength; physical qualities like Indra's arms as 'covered with hair' etc. (*Devatādhikaraṇa* IX, 1, 6-10). Although the *smṛti* texts are based on *mantra* and *arthavāda* texts, the latter two do not lend support to any notion that deities behave like or have qualities of human beings. There is neither any feeding of nor eating by any *devatā* in the case of sacrifices; in fact the deities never eat and are never intoxicated. They have no material body nor do they own anything.[41] Neither is there any proof by sense perception nor is there any textual evidence of an anthropomorphic view in the Vedic texts.

Deities are clearly distinguished from human beings, they cannot replace each other. In fact a deity is not even able to perform sacrifices[42] nor can man replace the deity to which the offerings are made in a sacrifice. Nevertheless deities are important for the performance of a sacrifice, "since the very term 'sacrifice' denotes an act bearing upon a substance and a deity" (G. JHA).[43] In the case of a conflict between the offering material, i.e. substance, and a deity the former is considered to be more important,[44] although the deity is always related to the sacrifice. Substance and deity are both accomplished entities, but the deity is spoken of only as a subordinated factor, because

41. Śā. Bhā. 9.1 9 3.2.37 9.1.9 (see text p. 136).

42. Śā. Bhā. 6.1.5: "It is not correct that the animals also are entitled (to perform sacrifices) - who is then entitled? - ...The deities are not (entitled to perform sacrifices), because there are no other deities (to whom they could offer the sacrifice). There cannot be offering to one's own self; in fact, that would not be an offering at all" (see text p. 136).

43. Śā. Bhā. 6.1.2 (see text p. 136).

44. Śā. Bhā. 8.1.32 (see text p. 136).

the deity does not give the *phala* (fruit, reward).[45] The sacrifice is for the sake of the specific deity that is involved and for which no substitute can be made. Any substitute in such a case would then serve a different purpose. Actually, the deity serves only the purpose of becoming the recipient of a specific offering.[46]

There is no doubt for Śabara that the *devatā* as the recipient of the offering is necessary for the sacrificial act in which and for which the *devatā's* presence is indicated in the relevant Vedic texts. However, "the only means of knowing objects is to realize that everything is as it is cognized to be"[47], but sense perception does not show any contact with the deity. Śabara, however, knows it only insofar as Vedic injunctions are concerned with it. He is aware of the deity through inference. The deity is not actually visible, but through its important function in the sacrifice it is concerned with the visible dimension of reality. *Devatā* cannot be compared with *artha* as a material object. Although *artha* belongs to the realm of visibility, it can have, nonetheless, a superior position to the *devatā*. Nor can *devatā* be compared with *svarga*. Although *svarga* belongs to the realm of invisibility, it is not, however, an accomplished entity like *devatā*.

With regard to the *devatā* as an *existing* entity Śābara Bhāṣya 10.4.23 is responsible for the view often held in the past and expressed by D.V. GARGE that "the deities further are not

---

45. Śā. Bhā. 9.1.9: "The deity is spoken as subordinate. The substance and the deity are in fact accomplished entities (i.e. already existing (*bhūtam*). ...

Though the sacrifice is meant for the sake of the deity, thereby it is not set aside that it is with respect to the result. Man is aiming at the result. Our activity is with a view to our purpose (i.e. man)—and not that of a deity" (see text p. 137).

46. Śā. Bhā. 6.3.18: "In case of a flaw as regards the deity, the fire, the *mantra* or the action, there can be no substitute (for the performance of a sacrifice)—why?—Because it is related to another purpose. A substitute would be different from those (original ones). Something different cannot serve the purpose for those". (see text p. 137) .

Śā. Bhā. 10.4.23 (see text p. 137).

47. Śā. Bhā. 1.1.5 (see text p. 127).

even believed to have any existence anywhere else except in the Vedic *mantras* that describe them (2)."[48] In this context Śabara points out that terms denoting time are found to be spoken of as 'deity' [*kāla* (time), *māsa* (month) and *saṃvatsara* (year)].[49] This speaks against the opinion that by the term 'deity' we understand those 'beings', Agni and the rest who are described in *Itihāsas* and *Purāṇas* as living in heaven.[50] Further he states, if its denotation were to rest entirely on the application in the mantra and the Brāhmaṇa texts, then the meaning of the terms would always remain unknown, inasmuch as the generic name 'deity' is scarcely used in common parlance. And he concludes that deities are those who are *Sūktabhāk* and *Havirbhāk*.[51] Then he explains :

> "In the performance of a sacrifice no form (*rūpeṇa*) of the *devatā* is present. By what means then ? Through the related *śabda*. Like the Adhvaryu gives manual assistance, so the *devatā* assists through *śabda*. According to (the injunction) 'the *Hoṭr* pours the '*lepa*' with both hands'—though (the assistance is) related to the hands—it is the *Hotṛ* himself who assists. So too the assistance of the *devatā* through the related *śabda* is to be understood. Though the *devatā* is enjoined as the one who assists, the inherence (*samavāya* of the *devatā*) in the sacrifice is still due to *śabda* (i.e. the related *śabda*, name)....
>
> But how ? There is the *śabda*, indeed, related to offering (*haviṣā*). Through this relation the object (*artha*) also will be there as *devatā*. The *devatā* is thus that which through *śabda* is in a proper relation to the offering. The act is recognized as being done in reference to the object denoted only when it is found that it is not possible for the action to take place in reference to the word. Here the word (*śabda*), however, is itself involved in what has to be done

48. GARGE, D.V., *Citations*, p. 12. FN 2: "Vide Śabara on JS 10.4.23 (p. 1824)".

49. Śā. Bhā. 10.4.23 (see text p. 137).

50. Śā. Bhā. 10.4.23 (see text p. 137).

51. Śā. Bhā. 10.4.23 (see text p. 137).

(with regard to the sacrifice). Consequently, *śabda* does not function with the aim of 'demonstrating or explaining' an object (i.e., *śabda* is inextricably in the act itself). ...

(The opponent then says) No doubt *śabda* itself operates (is in force) as *devatā* ?

(Śabara's answer) This will not lead to any confutation by us. For this view does not oppose our position. ..."[52]

The relevance of *śabda* with reference to *devatā* is clearly evident in the above passage. The insistence on the *devatā* being confined to the Vedic mantras and rites only is a rather hasty conclusion. Taking Śabara's view of language into consideration there is strictly speaking no need of such a restriction of the presence of *devatā*. However, according to Śābara Bhāṣya the deities exist, for example, with the Vedic sacrifice and M. BIARDEAU rightly points out,[53] they do not enrich human knowledge about the invisible. The deity belongs to the imperceptible things,[54] i.e., it cannot be apprehended in terms of a visible object. Thus one cannot speak of it in the same way, as if it would belong to the visible dimension of reality. Insofar as *devatā* belongs to the invisible dimension and insofar as Śābara Bhāṣya operates meaningfully only within man's experience, any discussion of *devatā* is bound to fall short of what the *devatā* actually is. Those who give more information about *devatā* with regard to the *mantra* and *arthavāda* texts look at the mere surface of the texts.[55] In other words, according to Śabara, "what cannot be spoken of (as an object of perception) cannot be the object of sense perception."[56] One cannot

---

52. Śā. Bhā. 10.4.23 (see text p. 137).

53. "It does not seem to be an exaggeration to say that the deities are hardly anything more than names with which one is but barely preoccupied. They have no existence except in the Vedic rites, and the *śruti* reveals them only with reference to the function of the sacrifices, like integral parts of the complex ritual. One cannot consider them as a particular object which can be taught for its own sake and which would enrich human knowledge of the invisible" (BIARDEAU, M., *Théorie*, p. 88).

54. Śā. Bhā. 1.1.5 (see text p. 127).

55. cf. Śā. Bhā. 9.1.9 (see text p. 138).

56. Śā. Bhā. 1.1.5 (see text p. 127).

speak of it, yet its presence cannot be denied either; nor can it be confined to a specific place, because *devāta* itself is involved through *śabda*.

(*iii*) *Apūrva*

Within the visible dimension of reality sense perception includes the awareness of change. By comparing entities with regard to similarities and differences man perceives objects in a sense of 'relative permanence'. For example, the material substance of the sacrifice is completely burnt and the remains are a new visible entity,[57] namely asheṣ ; or also grains have a new visible purpose in agricultural operations, namely for the production of new grains. Change cannot be perceived within an entity itself. Change itself is an act, "which transposes its substratum from one place to another" (G. JHA).[58] Hence no new qualities or structures become visible in an object, but there is a mere dislocation or removal in the external world. Whatever is actually perceived is only an accomplished entity, such as the necklace, the *svastika*, the dish etc.[59]

Within the invisible dimension of reality no sense perception provides us with any entity, i.e. we are not in contact with the invisible in the same way as we are with the visible. For example, at the sacrifice the *devatā* is present as an entity to which nothing is added for its accomplishment ; it is really present through the word, but is not perceived as an object itself. The fact of not actually perceiving the form of a *devatā* does not seem to undermine Śabara's view on *devatā*, because for him *devatā* still serves the function of (only) supporting the sacrificial act. What is noteworthy here with reference to Śabara's view on sacrifice and *devatā* is that the actual sacrifice, whose importance cannot be overemphasized, operates in the visible dimension of reality; in a sense the *devatā*, which belongs to the invisible dimension, is subservient to the performance of the sacrifice (though ultimately both *devatā* and the sacrifice are in a mutual relationship).

57. Śā. Bhā. 2.1.5 (see text p. 138).
58. Śā. Bhā. 2.1.5 (see text p. 138).
59. Śā. Bhā. 1.1.5 (see text p. 127).

In fact what poses a major problem with regard to the sacrifice is *svarga*. *Svarga* cannot be recognised as an entity even by the completion of the sacrifice. This is the case although the *mantra* were correctly recited and even when the material substançe under a correctly performed sacrificial act itself 'perishes'. No change as transposition of the visible sacrifice into *svarga* can be noticed, so that one could say that the invisible purpose "*svarga*" is achieved. There seems to be no link *prima facie* between sacrifice and heaven, although both are for man's benefit.

Śabara's views on the validity of the visible and invisible dimension of reality is at stake. Śabara does not introduce the concept of *time* as a reliable factor which accounts for the relation between the visible and invisible. Time does not appear as a creative or destructive power that can link events and entities in a certain chain of sequences and disruptions. In other words, the invisible result, "*svarga*", is not dependent on time for its achievement. Further Śabara does not take for granted any special reason for the non-perception of an invisible entity (for example, *svarga*). Rather he assumes an invisible force or power, called *apūrva*, which, as he says, necessarily escapes any sense perception.

The term "*apūrva*" itself[60] is a negative one, i.e. not "*pūrva*", but "apūrva". Hence the term excludes whatever visible content that may have been perceived in any previous and hitherto existing entity. For example *apūrva* is not the foreknown ashes that are a consequence of the sacrificial fire nor is it the foreknown fruit of grains or seeds used in agricultural operations. *Apūrva* (being literally the negation of *pūrva*) means that it does not connote any idea or notion of what is "previous", "former", "prior to", "preceding", or what has been "earlier" than what is now. In other words, *apūrva* cannot be foreseen in nor forecast by expressive terms nor known by description based on either sense perception or logic. Thus *apūrva* is unpreceded and unprecedented, it did not exist before and is thus quite new. It is also unparalleled and incomparable. *Apūrva* is an extraordinary power leading to an intended though unforeseen consequence

60. cf. MONIER-WILLIAMS, *Dictionary*, *apūrva* p. 65, col. 2 and *pūrva* p. 643, col. 1.

of a sacrificial act : heaven (*svarga*). In brief, " '*apūrva*' is what did not exist before, that which is new" (BIARDEAU).[61]

In fact according to Śabara there are no means by which one can describe what is denoted by *apūrva*. There is no insight into it by names,[62] i.e., nouns which are based on the contact with 'substances and qualities', which in fact belong to the visible dimension of reality. He says,

> "Thus there is a word which expresses this (sacrificial act) so that the *apūrva* is 'known'. Therefore we say that verbs (*bhāvaśabda* ; word of activity, becoming) incite the *apūrva*. But there is no word at all which actually expresses the *apūrva*... Therefore verbs (*karmaśabda*; verb of action) which have an object that comes into existence incite the *apūrva*."[63]

Therefore *apūrva* cannot be spoken of by denoting it through nouns. *Apūrva* remains invisible. Thus the emphasis has to be laid on verbs, which in fact do not denote anything in existence. They have an 'activity', especially, a 'becoming' or 'coming into existence', as their fundamental denotation.[64] *Apūrva* is comprehended as a result of an act[65] in the sense of completing the activity involved and of fulfilling the invisible purpose intended. It is embedded in the accomplishment, i.e., in the bringing about of what is desired *and* of what is enjoined in the sacrificial act. Thus it is not actually in existence yet, but is still an invisible purpose behind the act.

---

61. "*Apūrva* 'Ce qui n'existait pas auparavant, ce qui est nouveau'" (BIARDEAU, M., *Théorie*, p. 466).

G. JHA's translation of *apūrva* as 'Transcendental Potency' may be misleading on account of the various implications from the standpoint of Western Philosophy.

62. cf. Serial No. 15: Śā. Bhā. 2.1.3.

63. Śā. Bhā. 2.1.1 (see text p. 138).

64. Śā. Bhā. 2.1.4 (see text p. 138).

65. cf. *bhāvaśabda*: Śā. Bhā. 2.1.1 (see text p. 138).

Actually *apūrva* has its share in *bhāvanā*, i.e. in an "efficient force" (D'SA),[66] which is expressed by words (verbs) not only denoting an action, but expressing an activity (*bhāvanā*).[67] One can speak of *bhāvanā* only if there arises a real connection between the agent involved and the "doing or becoming" which is implied in the verb. In other words, the bringing into existence of *svarga* is due to this efficient force, called *bhāvanā*, insofar as it is connected with the agent desiring the particular result. This, however, does not imply that *bhāvanā* is only at work in or restricted to a sacrificial context, but it also operates in any activity in the visible world. *Bhāvanā* does indicate *apūrva*, insofar as it is embodied in words denoting activity (*bhāvārtha*). Nevertheless, in spite of logical and linguistic analysis one cannot call *apūrva* the causal link. Insofar as *bhāvanā* relates '*svargakāmaḥ*' and '*yajeta*', i.e. the connection between 'one desirous of heaven' and 'one should sacrifice', *apūrva* relates the invisible result (*svarga*) with the agent (*svargakāmaḥ*) who performs the sacrifice. However BIARDEAU's view,[68] that *apūrva* can be called a "mere relation" seems to be rather debatable. The efficient force (*bhāvanā*) which brings something new into existence (what has not been foreseen and known before or after a sacrificial act, i.e. *apūrva*) would become so weak that in fact *bhāvanā* would turn out to be only a superficial relation without being a force.

There is, according to Śabara, an *apūrva*, because the sacrificial act is perishable.[69] *Apūrva* is brought into existence by the act, to be more precise, by *bhāvanā*. That the act is perishable does not include that the efficient force has been annihilated

---

66. SA, F.D', Revelation without a God—Kumarila's Theory of Sabdapramanam, in: AMALORPAVADASS, D.S., (ed.), *Research Seminar on Non-Biblical Scriptures*, Bangalore, 1974, p. 478 (Quoted henceforth: SA, F.D.', *Revelation*.).

67. Śā. Bhā. 2.1.4 (see text p. 138).

68. "The *apūrva* charged with the task of relating the sacrificial act to its ultimate result is the minimum that he had to suppose in order to sustain his system in order to assure the unconditional validity of the revelation. One could say of it that it is a pure relation" (BIARDEAU, M., *Théorie*, p. 93).

69. Śā. Bhā. 2.1.5 (see text p. 139).

without having fulfilled its function. Words denoting activity (*bhāva*) do not stop their function by the mere utterance. Also the implication of doing or becoming in the verbs has not been limited by the perishing of the act without having brought something into existence. *Bhāvanā*, which is clearly recognizable through the conjugational affix of the term '*bhāvayet*' ('should bring into existence') denotes the human agent and the connected "bringing into existence". This gives support to the continuation and operation of what the implied result is, namely the fulfilment of the act. The immediate result of *bhāvanā* as the efficient force leading to the fulfilment of a sacrificial act is not the intended *svarga*, but *apūrva*. When an action is directed towards an invisible result (except when the action serves as a preparatory or a subservient purpose), there is *apūrva*. It is a result of *bhāvanā* too, that sacrificial materials have a function in the sacrificial act. No *apūrva* is involved in any function which produces only a visible result. Since the invisible *apūrva* comes into existence through *bhāvanā* by visible means, namely sacrificial material, the whole sacrificial act which perishes is presupposed. Thus the invisible is supported by *dṛṣṭa*, although this support does not last. In other words the *dṛṣṭa* has not the permanence which is required to bring into existence the desired result itself (*svarga*). Only *apūrva* actually comes into existence and *apūrva* cannot by any means be anticipated. Thus the support to *apūrva* by *dṛṣṭa* is only known by inference. It is perhaps more adequate to say that *apūrva* is due to the condition set by *dṛṣṭa* (i.e., *dravya* and man in a sacrificial act). In fact, since the desired *svarga* is not achieved by the mere completion of the sacrificial act, it might be said that a radically new aspect (*apūrva*) is involved through the sacrificial achievement. *Svarga* is only indirectly involved as the sacrificial aim. It has still to be achieved, as it is only enjoyed by the agent of the sacrificial act after death.

Apūrva has its own existence. It cannot be grasped or confined within the visible dimension of reality. Therefore the question about its existence or destruction, when *svarga* is realized is a futile one. All pros and cons for its permanent existence are mere speculation. In fact Śabara does not seem to be concerned about it. He only states, that *apūrva* cannot be considered as *ātman*, because *ātman* is already found everywhere. There is no possibility either of equating *apūrva* with *devatā* or *svarga*. Nonetheless the "existence" of *apūrva* comes about as soon as the track of the visibility is lost. And this above all is important to Śabara namely that this independent force *apūrva* exists for man's benefit through the awakening of the efficient force *bhāvanā*. In fact at each non-subservient act leading to an invisible result a "different" *apūrva* is at work. Each act has its own distinct *apūrva* with regard to an invisible result.[70] Hence *apūrva* does not come into existence unless there is the activity of the sacrifice. When *apūrva* is brought into existence by the proper functioning of the sacrificial act, one can say that *apūrva* is the result of the act. In fact there is an irony involved in the performance of the sacrifice : *apūrva* comes into existence (only) by fulfilling the sacrifice which includes the intended achievement of *svarga* as its fulfilment. But the existence of *svarga* cannot be spoken of with reference to the visible reality, nor can *svarga* be immediately beneficial to the sacrificer.

According to Śabara's view of reality the sacrifice seems to be the only act where we can discover a 'creative aspect' within the realm of visibility. One has to keep in mind that sense perception is usually in contact with a 'new entity' after an act has been carried out. The outcome of an act can be recognised in terms of similarity and of difference of entities needed for comparison. It is not so in the sacrificial act in spite of its being a transposition of the substratum from one place to the other. No comparison of entities is possible, because the result of the sacrificial act is invisible. Therefore it is only in this specific context that one can say that Śabara assumes something completely new, which could be called a 'creative aspect', namely *apūrva*. The only authority for this assumption is the Veda, which is *śabda*.[71] This 'creative aspect' is nothing else

70. cf. Śā. Bhā. 2.1.6-7: Śā. Bhā. 2.2.1 (see text p. 139).

71. cf. below pp. 70-84. Śā. Bhā. 2.1.6-7: "By '*codanā*' (as mentioned in the *sūtra*) we say there is *apūrva*. The *apūrva* exists because an action which is to be done is prescribed in the form of 'one who desires heaven should sacrifice'. Otherwise the injunction would not make any sense (or be without object)" (see text p. 139).

than the bringing about of the invisible (*svarga*). It has its basis in the sacrifice which is in the visible dimension of reality and the visible dimension is said to have a stable order. This stable order is somehow set aside by *apūrva* and hence it is called 'creative'. Something new arises, which has no equal in man's experience. Hence the invisible is 'revealed', but no new qualities hidden in an object or event are revealed. The visible and invisible are still two dimensions of reality and not of a particular object. The 'creative aspect' cannot be *bhāvanā* in general nor the sacrificial act in particular. One cannot speak of a human or divine being or power, which is creative, nor does *ātman* become a creative agent. Creativity is here equated with *apūrva,* which in being beyond sense perception is an invisible force.

Apūrva, the invisible power, not only overcomes the dualistic tension which is probably caused by the rational assumption of temporal and non-temporal or visible and invisible aspects of reality, but it also points to a dimension of reality which is not supposed either by *ratio* or by perception. No insight into *apūrva* is in fact possible. It cannot be perceived or spoken of. Its invisible power is expressed only negatively, i.e. as *apūrva,* not *pūrva.*

According to Śabara's explanation of reality, *apūrva* performs not only an indispensable function for man's benefit, but it is fundamental to his view of reality. If *apūrva* is considered to be a mere fiction, reality has only one dimension, namely *dṛṣṭa.* In Śabara's opinion, explanations of reality which exclude *apūrva,* face more difficulty than those faced by himself to explain the function of the sacrifice. Besides, *dharma,* his main interest would then become meaningless. Without *apūrva* the efforts to reach one's *dharma* would remain within an already established visible order of the universe. To obtain the highest good in such a way has no basis in experience and it will not be experienced unless one grants the existence of *apūrva.* Thus according to Śabara, *apūrva* has a real existence and function within reality. Both, *dṛṣṭa* and *adṛṣṭa* are real. If reality has only one dimension, one could say, it remains like a torso, i.e. incomplete and deprived of life. In other words reality is cut into parts, of which the visible ones give rise to invalid concepts of reality. The relevance of perception and *śabda* is thereby neither recognized nor understood.

3. *Assessment of the dṛṣṭa and the adṛṣṭa*

The visible dimension of reality, i.e., *dṛṣṭa,* indicates the significance of language in the sense that the reference to the object must be contained *really* and *not ideally*. Language cannot be a construction or production of the human mind. It is not an act of reproduction or image which is left behind by a sensory organ, because that cognition is real sense perception (*sat pratyakṣam*) which appears, when there is contact of the sense organs of a person with the object perceived (*tatsaṃprayoge*).[72] Hence language and its functioning cannot be based on something which is purely within us—an impression that has only to be expressed. For a supporter of Śabara this view of the visible rejects any ground for an idealistic (and metaphysical) view of language and for hermeneutics. However, a "just and correct view" of what is presented (*pratyakṣa*), which has its support in and from the object, seems to be fundamental to language. What seems to be obvious according to Śabara's view of the *dṛṣṭa,* which points to the *adṛṣṭa* dimension of reality, is that language cannot be a mere medium of communication, a transfer of ideas or even a product of the mechanism of speech.

The invisible dimension of reality, i.e., *adṛṣṭa* indicates also the significance of language in the sense that the reference to the invisible must obtain *really* and *not ideally*. *Adṛṣṭa* is within the realm of language, although it cannot be spoken of directly. There is no word which expresses *apūrva* (what did not exist before, what is new). One can only point to or indicate this invisible force by its negative term *apūrva.* Nevertheless *apūrva* is integrated in language through *bhāvanā* (efficient force), from which it can arise as something radically new and unforeseen. The explanation of *devatā,* whose presence is manifested only through the word (*śabda*), shows clearly that the *devatā*'s

72. Śā. Bhā. 1.1.5

presence is not within sense perception. Its presence, however, is no less significant in speech. *Svarga* (happiness/heaven), which is the desire of all men cannot be actually described in terms of speech. Nevertheless, its presence is supported by *apūrva* and is anticipated through the sacrificial act where it is not withheld within language in the sense that *svarga* is expressed as a wish of man and as a forthcoming result of the sacrifice.

As the *adṛṣṭa*, the invisible, is within the realm of language, language cannot be based only on the contact between man and an object which is bound to the visible. In other words, language is not only structured by sense perception which has no direct access to *adṛṣṭa*. The sacrificial act wherein *adṛṣṭa* is present and 'at work' through the *devatā* and *apūrva*, indicates that language cannot be analysed in terms proper to the information theory of language, which consists:

> "in the reporting of events, the description of objects, the formulation of theoretical hypotheses, the statement of experimental findings and the handling of data."[73]

The information theory of language presupposes only sense perception, in which *adṛṣṭa* cannot be accounted for. All information strictly speaking, belongs to the dimension of visibility, i.e. based on finite media which are not *adṛṣṭa*. On the other hand, there is no indication in Śābara Bhāṣya which could lead to the assumption that language has its origin in *adṛṣṭa*. Neither *apūrva* nor *devatā* create language. Besides Śabara's explanation of *devatā* does not support the view that language is divine.

What comes to the fore in this analysis of reality is that *pratyakṣa* is only in direct contact with the visible dimension of reality, while language encompasses both dimensions of reality, *dṛṣṭa* and *adṛṣṭa*. The fact that *śabda* is directly related

---

73. LADRIERE, J., The Performativity of Liturgical Language, in: *Concilium* 2 (1973) No. 9, pp. 50-62, p. 51.

to both these dimensions is of crucial importance for Śabara in understanding reality. It has hermeneutical consequences. The way in which the hermeneutical problem comes into the right focus depends on Śabara's view of language. In other words, does an assessment of language present Śabara's view of reality ? Thus it is important how to understand Śabara's view of reality through the assessment of language.

CHAPTER III

ŚABARA'S VIEW OF LANGUAGE : ŚABDA AND ITS CHARACTERISTICS

The investigation into *dṛṣṭa* and *adṛṣṭa* as they are presented by Śabara, seems to rule out any possibility of any existence which is beyond the reality which he speaks of. Reality itself is within the reach of language which cannot be apart from this reality itself. This is the case because for Śabara the two dimensions of reality as *dṛṣṭa* and *adṛṣṭa* entail and encompass everything. Nonetheless for Śabara the question of reality is not a simple problem. It is complex insofar as his explanation rests not only on sense perception (*pratyakṣa*), but is also based on the Vedas which are recognised by him as *śruti* ('hearing', 'revelation'). Hence, his explanation of reality and language has already presumed the function of language itself and this is the major problem Śabara is faced with. The validity of his thesis on *dharma* is entirely based on the Veda, when he supports the *sūtra* :

> "*Dharma* is the object that is indicated by thc Vedic injunctions."[1]

According to Śābara Bhāṣya one actually knows *dharma*, "because there is 'instruction' (*upadeśa*); instruction stands for the speaking of a particular set of words."[2] One also knows acts which are not known by sense perception and other means of knowledge, as for example, *anumāna* (inference), *upamāna* (comparison), *arthāpatti* (presumption) and *abhāva* (negation,

1. Mī. sū. 1.1.2 (see text p. 127).
2. Śā. Bhā. 1.1.5 (see text p. 127).

non-existence, absence),[3] but only through instruction, i.e. it ultimately implies Vedic injunction. Hence one could say that the understanding of reality and especially the knowledge of *dharma* and whatever is not visible ultimately falls within the function of language. Language is the primordial mystery on which Śabara throws some light through his careful explanation of *śabda*. *Śabda* is the focus of the whole problem of reality and language and ironically it is the key to the problem of reality and language. Thus it is of no less importance for hermeneutics.

1. *Śabda*

The incapability of translating *śabda* into another language by a single term is the main difficulty of any investigation into *śabda*. Hence various terms in English may illuminate some aspects of *śabda* and only the comprehension of *all* these terms together leads to an understanding of the inherent multidimensional meaning of the single word '*śabda*'. Consequently *śabda* can be represented especially by the terms 'sound', 'noise' and 'speech', but *śabda* also connotes terms such as 'phoneme', 'vowel', 'word', 'resonance', 'language' (primordial and human), 'unity of sense/signs/language', 'manifestation of a word' etc. A few examples of the many found in Śābara Bhāṣya may briefly illustrate the complex use of *śabda* :

śabda : sound/phoneme/word as physical reality
"The *śabda* may be the product of air (*vāyukāraṇaka*): in fact it is air which, through certain conjunctions and disjunctions, becomes the *śabda*"[4]

śabda : noise, sound
"*śabdaṃ kuru*" (make a noise, produce a sound)[5]

śabda : phoneme

---

3. Cf. Śā. Bhā. 1.1.5. The quotation of the Vṛttikāra in this context suggests that Śabara has endorsed the view of Vṛttikāra who refers to six *pramāṇas*.

G.P. BHATT has already pointed out "that Dr. Jha's rendering of the term '*upamāna*' as 'analogy' is quite misleading" (*Epistemology* pp. 293-294).

4. Śā. Bhā. 1.1.22 (see text p. 139). cf. also Śā. Bhā. 1.1.6-7, 13,15, 17.

5. Śā. Bhā. 1.1.14 (see text p. 139). cf. also Śā. Bhā. 1.1.8.

"It is another phoneme, (*varṇāntaram*)" says the *sūtra* 1.1.16, but Śabara comments : "The *y* is another *śabda* as the *i*" (*śabdāntaram*).[6]

śabda : word, term
"the word cow" (*go śabda*)[7]

śabda : phoneme, 'what is heard', term
"Among the people the term *śabda* (*śabdaśabdaḥ*) is applied to what is apprehended by the ear; and in this case the said letters (i.e. a reference to *ga-kāra* etc.) are what are apprehended by the ear"[8] (cf. Śabara speaks of '*varṇa*' and '*pada*' in the same context).

śabda : sound, vowel, noise, resonance (which is not accepted by Śabara), term
"It has been argued by the opponent that 'when several people are beating the *bherī* (drum) or pronounce a word (sound, vowel; i.e. raise their voice) (*śabdam*), one perceives a big noise (*mahāñ-śabda*) and one concludes there is an augmentation of the particles of sound (*śabda*) with each person. In fact it is not so. *Śabda* has no parts as it is shown by the fact that we cannot perceive a division of parts and as it (namely *śabda*) is without parts, no (variable) extension of it is possible. Hence there is no augmentation of *śabda*. It is soft (when pronounced)by one man, when there are several people these same phonemes (*akṣarāṇi*), on account of being taken up continuously by conjunctions and disjunctions (ripples) which fill all the space in the ear-cavity, come to be heard as 'augmented', and having parts. The conjunctions and disjunctions which are produced continuously in such a way and manifest *śabda* are denoted by the term *nāda* (resonance) (*nādaśabdavācyāḥ*). Hence the augmentation

6. Śā. Bhā. 1.1.16 (see text p. 139).
7. Śā. Bhā. 1.1.20 (see text p. 139).
8. Śā. Bhā. 1.1.5 (see text p. 127).

(mentioned above) depends on resonance and not on *śabda*."[9]

śabda : mere enunciation; permanent unity
"The *śabda* (pronounced) yesterday has perished". Śabara opposes this view and shows *śabda* as a unity of signs/sense/language, "because it has not perished."[10]

The difficulty of translating a text from one language into another is only an extreme case of the problem of communication itself. Communication is not a mere problem of the correct mastery of language, but one of accurate mutual understanding which takes place through the medium of a language.[11] A classical example of the problem of communication and understanding in its relation to language as such is found in Śābara Bhāṣya in a very complex discussion over *śabda*. The opponent of Śabara often insists on *śabda* as a physical reality, whereas Śabara speaks of *śabda* as a signifying unit. One gets the impression that two different levels of speech are presupposed, although there is no distinction in Śābara Bhāṣya between the ontological presumption of the opponent and the epistemological one of Śabara. Consequently the focus of *śabda* seems to have converged arguments that are apparently based on different levels from which different aspects of *śabda* are explained. However, the problem of communication with reference to the ontological and epistemological levels is not directly noticed in the elaborate discussion on *śabda* in Śābara Bhāṣya. Śabara and his opponent discuss the question of *śabda* in such a way that although in general both of them speak of *śabda*, yet in particular each presents different aspects of *śabda*.

9. Śā. Bhā. 1.1.17 (see text p. 139).
10. Śā. Bhā. 1.1.20 (see text p. 140).
11. With reference to philosophical translations N.S.S. RAMAN significantly points out: "...broadly speaking, translations are interpretations and interpretations are translations. ... it is a mistake to suppose that given mastery of two languages, one could effortlessly translate from one language to the other, even supposing at the same time, that the translator has a sound philosophical knowledge". (RAMAN, N.S.S., The Problem of Philosophical Translation, in *Indian Philosophical Annual*, Vol. VII, 1971, 1-14, p. 3.)

It seems that one would misinterpret Śabara's view of *śabda*, if one splits the epistemological and ontological dimensions, or if one ignores some aspects of the multidimensional meaning of *śabda* in Śabara's explanation. A distinction between 'thought' and 'being itself' made in any analysis is a mere construction for Śabara, because for him no being-in-itself (in the Western sense) can be cognised. Things are as they are cognised[12] and cognition through inference is based on a perceived relationship.[13] There is no reliability, if one separates 'thought' from 'being', if one distinguishes between ontology and epistemology as separate levels each having its own independent value and function. One cannot trace in Śābara Bhāṣya the ontological-epistemological distinction which arises from discursive thought. Besides the opponent's view of *śabda* is on the *dṛṣṭa*-level of reality. According to Śabara, *śabda* cannot be comprehended in its multidimensionality unless considered with reference to reality as a whole, which for him includes the *adṛṣṭa*. In this sense the opponent's view of *śabda* falls short of an adequate representation of the multidimensional *śabda* in not taking into account the *adṛṣṭa*. What is important to note is that *śabda* cannot be split into a physical reality or into a signifying unit, but that it encompasses both aspects as a consequence of which it obtains its inherent multidimensionality.

2. *The autpattika, nitya, apauruṣeya* Characteristics

According to Mī. sū. 1.1.5 "the relation between *śabda* and (its) object is *autpattika*."[14] The derivation of *autpattika* from *ut-patti* (arising, birth, production, origin)[15] indicates that the term *autpattika* is confined to production and birth, for

---

12. Śā. Bhā. 1.1.5 (see text p. 127).

13. Śā. Bhā. 1.1.5 (see text p. 127). G.P. BHATT points out: "Śabara's definition of inference should be formulated thus: 'When the perception of one term of a well-known relationship leads to the cognition of the other term of that relationship, which latter is not in contact with the person's sense-organs, this second cognition is called inference'" (*Epistemology*, p. 207).

14. Mī. sū. 1.1.5 (see text p. 127).

15. MONIER-WILLIAMS *Dictionary*, p. 180 col. 3.

example, if a word denotes an object, then the relation between *śabda* and object is immediately born. In other words, the relation between *śabda* and the object or vice versa is originally existent, namely it is *autpattika.* Although the term *autpattika* points clearly to the origin of any object with reference to *śabda* and vice versa, there is no evidence that the term *autpattika* in this context involves any human or divine creativity nor does it suggest that this original relation has to be considered as being eternal. Śabara comments on this relation:

> "*Autpattika*—what we mean by this is '*nitya*'. It is 'origin' that is indirectly spoken of as existence (presence). It is the existence, inseparable from the word and the object, that constitutes the relation and there is no relation (made, constituted) after both of them have been produced."[16]

In other words, *autpattika* points to an understanding of the origin of *śabda* and *artha* (object) in the sense that both of them are brought about simultaneously. There is no connection (*saṃbandha*) by subsequently attributing *śabda* to an object or vice versa. There is not initially a being and subsequently *śabda* or vice versa with reference to objects. Whenever *śabda* is present, then whatever is related to it exists as well. Everything originates in and with *śabda* and not through any general agreement or consent, i.e. *śabda* does not rely on convention. It is insignificant, whether the object of *śabda* belongs to the visible or invisible dimension of reality. Although the invisible cannot be spoken of as perceptible, nonetheless it is related to *śabda,* because the realm of *śabda* operates beyond the realm of sense perception. *Śabda* and its object are co-existent in and through their immediate and inborn relation. *Śabda,* insofar as it inevitably connotes an object, is in this sense *autpattika.*

In the above quotation it is evident that Śabara mentions another characteristic of the *śabda*/object relation, namely *nitya.* BIARDEAU makes a very valuable comment in this context:

> "The term *nitya* does here not connote eternity nor does it even specifically refer to permanence; one would be more

16. Śā, Bhā. 1.1.5 (see text p. 128).

tempted to evoke its original sense as 'proper', 'personal', equivalent to *sva*, as Hara has well enlightened us on the matter (2); then *nitya* would designate more a kind of extrinsic appropriation, the strictly parallel formation of two entities with a different nature, than an internal exigency—*svābhāvika*—of the object that would require the word."[17]

Consequently in this context the term *nitya* does not seem primarily to point out any qualification of existence in terms of time or the exclusion of the latter, but it stresses emphatically that *śabda* is never outside of or apart from the *autpattika* relation. Whereas the Nyāya-Vaiśeṣika view for example assumes a substance being deprived of any quality in its first moment of existence, Śabara strictly excludes any process, which is actually analysed in 'discontinued moments' and which might lead to or deprive *śabda* of the *autpattika* relation at a certain stage. It seems that for Śabara it is proper (*nitya*) to *śabda* and the object (*artha*) that they are in an *autpattika* relation which belongs especially (*nitya*) to the very nature of both of them. *Śabda*, insofar as it inevitably connotes the *nitya* characteristic of the *śabda*/object relation, can itself be characterised as *nitya*.

A third characteristic is mentioned in the same context. "The relation between *śabda* and the object is *apauruṣeya*."[18] In fact "when *śabda* is known, the object is known."[19] There is no intermediary function needed to establish this relation. It is a natural connection which is *autpattika* and *nitya*. Thus Śabara refutes the argument that this relation is created or produced by anyone and calls it *apauruṣeya*. *Apauruṣeya* indicates that it has no human source. It is obvious that Śabara does not mean divine by *apauruṣeya*, as it can be seen from his explanation of *devatā*.[20] Nor does he use the term *puruṣa* as encompassing gods and men, as it can be seen from the use of the term by ṛṣis. There is no doubt that in Śābara Bhāṣya the

17. BIARDEAU, M., *Théorie*, pp. 156-157.
18. Śā. Bhā. 1.1.5 (see text p. 128).
19. Śā. Bhā. 1.1.5 (see text p. 128).
20. cf. above Chapt. II, See 2 (ii)

term *apauruṣeya* means neither human nor divine. *Śabda*, insofar as one cannot trace any creation with regard to the relation between *śabda* and object, is in this sense *apauruṣeya.*

Although *śabda* is clearly characterised by its relation with the object it refers to and is consequently characterised by *autpattika, nitya* and *apauruṣeya,* Śabara further clarifies the characteristic of *śabda* in its relation to what may be called *origin* and *function.*

According to Śabara the assumption of a creator or promulgator of the *autpattika/nitya* relation is untenable. The thesis about the relation being *autpattika* "is established, because the relation cannot be the work of anyone (*apauruṣeyatvāt*)."[21] In fact Śabara mentions especially that nobody can remember any creator of the relationship between *śabda* and its object.[22] Besides "a certain usage becomes possible, only when there is an agreement between the creator and the adopter of the usage and not when there is disagreement between them."[23] Furthermore Śabara says that technical terms coined by Pāṇini and Piṅgala are not based on any natural relation, but that they are artificially coined. They cannot be understood without reference to the specific use of the technical terms by the authors concerned. Śabara refers to Pāṇini's *sūtra* 1.1.1. : "The term *vṛddhi* stands for the letters *āt* and *aic*" as a good illustration of such conventional relationship, where the object '*āt-aic*' of the term *vṛddhi* (*vṛddhiśabda*) cannot be understood apart from the specific reference to the use of the terms as coined/created by the author, i.e. the relation between *vṛddhi* and the vowels

---

21. Śā. Bhā. 1.1.5 (see text p. 128).

22. S. MURTY adds: "His immediate commentator, Śabara, commenting on that *sūtra,* says that just as the Himālayas are not remembered to have been made by anyone, words and their relations also were not fixed by anyone. This implies that like the Himālayas (and the world), words and their meanings are natural and uncreated. We are left to conjecture whether Śabara believed in a God who is not a creator, or in a supreme Ātman." (*Revelation,* p. 190).

However, it may be said with reference to the invisible dimension of reality that Śabara did not and could not point out any divine function of a creator.

23. Śā. Bhā. 1.1.5 (see text p. 128).

ā ai, au cannot be understood without reference to the use of them by Pāṇini himself.[24] However, it would be absurd to accept that a certain convention is based on one or many (creative) authors at the same time, so that the relation would receive a universal acceptance at any place.[25] Besides this convention cannot be communicated apart from *śabda* which is thereby presupposed.[26] To Śabara it seems impossible that such a creator of the relation could have been forgotten and even if that would be the case, he says, "we could not admit a creator of the relation unless there were proofs for it."[27] His argument is mainly based on his perception of the use of language, where he says :

> "One teaches (the relation) as something already established (siddha)."[28]
>
> "One sees when adults use words for their object (or for their purpose) that the children listen and recognize directly the object (in front of their eyes). When these adults were young, they (learnt it) from other adults and those again from others; there is no beginning (to this process)."[29]
>
> "There is never a moment when the relation has been totally absent, (i.e.,) when a *śabda* has never been related to any object. —Why so ? —Because the creation of the relation would be impossible itself. One who creates a relation necessarily makes use of some word in order to create it. Who would have created (the relation) of this (word) which he would make use of ? If one says, somebody else has created it, then by whom is that one (made) and again that one ? One does not reach any end. Who has created a relation therefore must admit necessarily that there are some words of which the relation has not been

24. Śā. Bhā. 1.1.5 (see text p. 128).
25. Śā. Bhā. 1.1.5 (see text p. 128).
26. Śā. Bhā. 1.1.5 Serial No. 30.
27. Śā. Bhā. 1.1.5 (see text p. 128).
28. Śā. Bhā. 1.1.5 (see text p. 128).
29. Śā. Bhā. 1.1.5 (see text p. 129).

created and they are already (established) in the usage of the adults."[30]

Although all the reasons pointed out by Śabara seem to be concerned with the non-existence of any creative function by which one can conclude a conventional relation between *śabda* and its object, he himself gives evidence only for a permanent use of *śabda* and its related object. He shows thereby that *śabda* has a referential capacity which is not at random. No creator of the relation between *śabda* and its object appears in this permanent usage. Thus one cannot say that the relation has been established by anyone at any time. Śabara shows positively only the referential capacity of *śabda* and its object, and this does not necessitate the eternity or permanence of the said relation itself. Permanence, however, may be said to underly his explanation.

However, it is noteworthy that Śabara denies *śabda* as a mere sign which is operative by virtue of being within a system of signs and symbols produced by anyone. This can be seen clearly from his example of Pāṇini as the originator of technical terms. Consequently the assumption that the *autpattika/nitya* relation bears the characteristic of being *apauruṣeya* remains valid for Śabara and characterises *śabda* itself. Hence origin and function of *śabda* are never within any human or divine creativity or productivity, i.e. always within *apauruṣeyatvam*, based on his experience of the permanent use of the *śabda/* object relation.

3. *The Role of ākṛti and of the Specific Set of Phonemes*

The characteristics of *śabda* with regard to function and origin are further explained by referring to the object which is related to *śabda*. It is evident that Śabara excludes the view that the proper object of *śabda* could be an idea of a thing,[31] although this is implied by Śabara's opponent who argues:

"By their nature object and *śabda* (*śabdārthau*) are not related because of the fact that we perceive *śabda* (word) in the

30. Śā. Bhā. 1.1.5 (see text p. 129).
31. cf. above p. 42.

mouth (i.e. being pronounced) and the object on the ground (i.e. without affecting one's mouth, without permanent relation) and because people clearly make such a distinction as 'this is a word (śabda) and not the object (*artha*), this is the object, not the word (*śabda*)' and because there is a difference of form : one pronounces the word 'cow' (*gaur iti imaṃ śabdam*) and one understands an object with dewlap etc."[32]

Śabara spares no effort to show that the object is not a production conjured up by the mind, but that the object is necessarily related to and not separated from *śabda* and from reality itself. When he refers to the object, he introduces the term *ākṛti* ('specific form'—BIARDEAU, 'Gestalt'—FRAUWALLNER) :

> "What is the object of the word 'cow' ? We say it is the (specific) form—*ākṛti*—particularized by the dewlap etc."[33]

For Śabara the proper object of *śabda* is *ākṛti*. *Ākṛti* is neither the class (*jāti*) nor the individual (*vyakti*).[34] According to Śabara *ākṛti* cannot be separated from nor equated with the class and the individual. However, it is important to note that Śabara always maintains that *ākṛti* as proper object is permanently related to *śabda*,[35] i.e. *ākṛti* coexists with *śabda* and

---

32. Śā. Bhā. 1.1.5 (see text p. 129).

33. Śā. Bhā. 1.1.5 (see text p. 129).

34. M. BIARDEAU shows in a convincing way that it is *not* clear that the early Mīmāṃsā held the view that the meaning of a word refers to the universal and not to the individual. However, F. D'SA is correct, insofar as he says: "It is Kumārila who for the first time explains what this *ākṛthiḥ* (=universal) is. "It (is the species (=*jāti*-) (that) men call *ākṛtiḥ*, (namely that) through which an individual is substantially formed (*ākṛyate*) ...' (*SV* Ākṛtivādaḥ v3-4ab)" (see text p. 140). (SA, F.D', Ākṛtivādaḥ: The meaning of a word is per se universal, in: *Revelation* p. 476).

Nonetheless, one cannot say that *jāti* and *ākṛti* are the same for Śabara, as M. BIARDEAU has shown in her erudite study "*L'object du mot*, in: BIARDEAU, M., *Théorie*, pp. 161-177.

35. Śā. Bhā. 1.1.19: "Whenever the word 'cow' (*gośabda*) is uttered there is a notion of all the cows. From this it follows that (we say) it denotes the (specific) form (*ākṛti*). And it is not possible to create the relation

is not dependent on any conventional relation. It is interesting to see that *ākṛti* is actually perceived.[36] Consequently it is something which is accomplished (*siddha*)[37] and known in the realm of perception as well.

Actually what happens is that the specific form, namely *ākṛti*, is known in every case of perception, for example with reference to cows as a class or as individuals, as is pointed out in Śābara Bhāṣya 1. 1. 19.[38] In a very complex discussion (Śā. Bhā. 1. 3. 33) he points out that *ākṛti* is present and represented through *viśeṣaṇa*[39] which could be translated as a distinguishing, qualifying factor, which enables us to cognize the individual object (for example dewlap etc. as characteristic of cow). Śabara says that any specific object is known, because one already knows *viśeṣaṇa*, i.e. *ākṛti*. In the context of language *ākṛti* is the direct and proper object of *śabda*, "because the word (*śabda*) is the reason (*nimittam*) for the cognition of the (specific) form (*ākṛti*) and the cognition of *ākṛti* is the reason for the cognition of the individual."[40] Consequently *ākṛti* is the distinguishing factor of various objects and on account of this it simultaneously integrates the individual specified objects into a class (*jāti*), by which *ākṛti* gets the feature of being *sāmānya*, i.e. being a common feature of a class. In other words *ākṛti* as the qualifying factor functions in a comprehensive way whereby the individual is recognised. Thus it functions in an extensive way as an integrating factor to enable the view of a

---

between the word and the (specific) form (*ākṛtyā śabdasya*). Because the creator would establish the relation after having pointed out the *ākṛti*; or there are many forms within an individual cow (lit. the body of a cow). How will he indicate the separated form which is to be expressed by the word cow without having a word? If however the word cow is permanent (*nitya*), when it is spoken out several times as it has been previously heard as applied to other individual cows, it makes known by positive and negative concomitance that it expresses the (specific) form (cow). For this reason also it is *nitya*" (see text p. 140).

36. Śā. Bhā. 1.3.33 (Serial No. 41).
37. Śā. Bhā. 1.1.5 (see text p. 129).
38. Śā. Bhā. Serial No. 35.
39. Śā. Bhā. 1.3.33 (see text p. 140).
40. Śā. Bhā. 1.3.33 (see text p. 140).

specific class of specified individuals. *Ākṛti*, consequently, determines both the individual and the class. However, *ākṛti* is always concrete insofar as it is never isolated from the individual with which it is in real contact, i.e., it does not exist as a mere form of thought which could give rise to an erroneous cognition of an individual or a class. *Ākṛti* as the proper object of *śabda* is in contact with *śabda* and the individual object according to Śabara :

> "One cannot say, if the *ākṛti* is known through the word (*śabda*), that the individual is object of the word as well (*padārtha*), —Why ? —This is because the *ākṛti* is always in relation with the individual (*nityasaṃbaddha*) and when one of the terms of the relation, *ākṛti*, is known (*avagatāyām*) then the other term is known as well (*avagamyate*). This is evident in itself that if a word (*śabda*) is spoken out, an individual is known. But is it known from the word (*śabda*) or the (specific) form (*ākṛti*) ? The distinction is not directly perceivable. It becomes intelligible through similarity and difference. One who cognises the *ākṛti* even without the word (*antareṇāpi śabdam*) he necessarily cognises the individual whilst one who, affected by a mental derangement, will not grasp anything of the *ākṛti*, when the word (*śabda*) is uttered, he will not cognise the individual either."[41]

Hence, Śabara makes it very clear that if *ākṛti* is known (*avagatāyām*), then the related and corresponding part, namely the individual, is also known (*avagamyate*). Consequently the *viśeṣaṇa* (specific characteristic) which is *ākṛti* is by its very nature related to concrete reality. There is no doubt for Śabara that *ākṛti* is real. Its imperceivability occurs when there is a mental defect which results in erroneous perception. There is a close link between language and perception through the object (*ākṛti*) of *śabda*, but the cognition of any individual object itself is always due to this *ākṛti*. In other words there is neither

---

41. Śā. Bhā. 1.3.33 (see text p. 140).

perception nor language which necessarily relies on *śabda* without the (specific) form, i.e. *viśeṣaṇa/ākṛti*. Whatever can be distinguished and qualified (*viśeṣya*) can be pointed out by the (specific) form (*ākṛti/viśeṣaṇa*), although the latter cannot be separated from the distinguished entity itself (*viśiṣṭa*), since one who knows the *ākṛti* knows the individual.[42]

In fact constant use of *śabda* (word) and experience helps in the understanding of what the *ākṛti* is, since *ākṛti* is within the realm of perception. The specific form is always present, whenever *śabda* and/or perception is a means of knowledge. Although the use of *śabda* illustrates that *śabda* manifests the *ākṛti* and not the individual object, it does not at all mean that either *śabda* or *ākṛti* depends on the actual individual usage or experience.[43] *Śabda*, for example, is applied even to a newborn calf which has never been seen before, nor has the word 'cow' (*gośabda*) been applied previously to the newborn calf. "This is why it is impossible to resort to actual usage in order to say that the word cow expresses the individual" (*gośabdo vyaktivacana*).[44] This emphasizes that for Śabara the object of *śabda* does not depend on actual experience. If this were not the case then *śabda* would depend on experience and as a consequence of this *śabda* would not only rely on convention, but would also lead to inconsistency as in the case of *śabda* with reference to cow/calf.

This view of *ākṛti* seems neither to contradict nor to surpass Śabara's explanation of perception nor his outline of the *autpattika, nitya and apauruṣeya* relation between *śabda* and *artha* (object). *Ākṛti* is not another object as against or opposed to *artha*, nor is it only a subordinate part of the object (*artha*) related to *śabda* itself. The way in which Śabara illuminates *artha* is by explaining *ākṛti* as the proper object of *śabda*. Moreover only nouns, which are capable of expressing entities, indicate the realm of visibility (*dṛṣṭa*) and hence injunctive words do not and cannot express the proper object, namely *ākṛti*.[45]

---

42. Śā. Bhā. 1.3.33 (see text p. 140).
43. Śā. Bhā. 1.3.33 (see text p. 141).
44. Śā. Bhā. 1.3.33 (see text p. 141).
45. Śā. Bhā. 1.3.16 (see text p. 141).

Consequently insofar as the *dṛṣṭa* dimension of reality is concerned, it is evident for Śabara that reality is presented by *ākṛti* only through nouns. However, a problem seems to arise with regard to the *adṛṣṭa* dimension of reality since Śabara does not seem to throw any light on *ākṛti* in its function in the *adṛṣṭa* dimension. Hence *prima facie* one may draw several conclusions with reference to *ākṛti* and the *adṛṣṭa* dimension of reality : a) Śabara considers *ākṛti* irrelevant to the *adṛṣṭa* dimension, b) that *ākṛti* does not at all exist in the *adṛṣṭa* dimension, c) that *ākṛti* does not in fact operate in the *adṛṣṭa* dimension or d) that in the *adṛṣṭa* dimension the function or role of *ākṛti* is ineffable. However, what is important to bear in mind at this stage is that Śabara mentions objects of the *adṛṣṭa* dimension using nouns like *devatā*, *svarga*, *karman* etc.; moreover one has to recall as well Śabara's view of the *apauruṣeya* relation between *śabda* and its object :

> "With regard to an imperceivable object for example deity etc. it is useless and impossible to create a name (*saṃjñā*). Proper names in fact are made in order to know (things) in their particular features (*viśeṣa*) and in reference to these particularities (*viśeṣāṃś coddiśya*). When the particularities are unknown, both is (considered to be) impossible. Consequently the relation between the word and the object (śabdasya arthena) is *apauruṣeya*."[46]

According to Śabara it is futile to look for any conventional effort with regard to the origin of the relation, as it would involve a distinct knowledge of an object of the invisible dimension of reality. Actually the specific, particular distinction (*viśeṣa*) is a constituent element of creating this relation. *Viśeṣa* (specific, particular form) and *saṃjñā* (its proper name) do not bear any visible and experienceable ground for anyone who would create the mutually corresponding relation with regard to the *adṛṣṭa* dimension of reality.[47] For example *devatā* is not

---

46. Śā. Bhā. 1.1.5 (see text p. 129).

47. cf. for example Śabara's explanation of *agni/fire* and *agni/devatā*, see above pp. 25-27.

known in the *adṛṣṭa* dimension of reality as a consequence of which any specific form and name is unreliable in the human endeavour, which pretends to know the invisible object which is not within sense perception. However, Śabara does not say that *śabda* has no *viśeṣa,* i.e. there is no *ākṛti* in the *adṛṣṭa* dimension, but it is evident that *ākṛti* cannot be perceived and consequently cannot be spoken of in a distinct particular way. Nonetheless Śabara maintains that there is a relation between *śabda* and its object in both the *dṛṣṭa* and *adṛṣṭa* dimensions and calls the relation *apauruṣeya. Ākṛti* as a specific form of the invisible dimension cannot be discussed, because it is imperceivable and hence not at our disposal for purposes of description. However, Śabara sees no reason to abandon completely *ākṛti, adṛṣṭa* or *śabda.* Moreover, he sees no reason to explain the *ākṛti* of *devatā* in any concrete way, simply because there is no concrete information available apart from their presence in and through *śabda. Śabda* has its support in the invisible as is known from inference based on perception in the visible dimension of reality. Thus Śabara does neither bind nor restrict *śabda* and its object to the manifested and experienceable world which is only one dimension of reality as a whole. In fact he does not and cannot deny *ākṛti* for the *adṛṣṭa* dimension without restricting *śabda* only to the *dṛṣṭa* dimension. This conforms with his view that if there is any available reason for anything to exist, then its existence cannot be denied even though it cannot be perceived. However, it is evident for him that one cannot describe the invisible; the *ākṛti* of the invisible dimension is not at our disposal in which sense it is ineffable.

> BIARDEAU clearly characterises *ākṛti,* when she points out: "The *ākṛti* ('specific form') appears so like a privileged support of the word in the real, but on the other hand language, which is 'already there' as such, is the only means to refer to it practically in a safe way. It is the real, the most pregnant and to such an extent that one can perceive it even on the level of the individual. .."[48]

---

48. BIARDEAU, M., *Théorie,* p. 165.

BIARDEAU further characterizes *ākṛti* as being a "mediator between the real in general and human activity" and also as a "mediator between men and the entire expression through language."[49] This point is well made and leaves no doubt that language with reference to *śabda* and *ākṛti* has an instrumental character of mediation, but one has to be careful not to overstress *ākṛti* as mediator. An overemphasis on *ākṛti* as a mediating function simplifies and falsifies the view of *ākṛti* as proper object and *śabda* as signifying unit. In fact *ākṛti* with regard to language would function on its own and *śabda* would possess merely a referential capacity for *ākṛti* as the mediator. In other words, *śabda* becomes only a means which contains the mediating *ākṛti* and serves only as an analytical function to show the theoretical and practical value of *ākṛti*. An overemphasis on the practical mediating function of *ākṛti* seems to have only a theoretical value of *śabda*. Hence with regard to language it would mean that we are aware of *ākṛti* through experience and inference (based on perception)[50] and that it would function as mediator independently of *śabda*. In analytically investigating *ākṛti* and *śabda* one can trace a mediating function of *ākṛti*, but it does not give evidence of the fact that *ākṛti* alone is the mediator between *śabda* and reality on the one hand and human involvement on the other. One has to bear in mind that *ākṛti* is related to *śabda* and the individual object. It is on account of this relation that one can conclude that *ākṛti* is a presence which itself is real, though its presence cannot be perceived like an object which is at hand. Consequently and on account of the fact that the whole realm of *śabda* cannot be perceived, one cannot attribute the mediating function primarily either to *śabda* or *ākṛti*. The mediating function however seems to lie within the *relation* of *śabda* and *ākṛti*. With regard to language, there seems to be a mutual response between the two on

49. BIARDEAU, M., *Théorie*, p. 165-166.

50. cf. Śā. Bhā. 1.1.5: "(The inference) or relation is known through direct perception, e.g., where one knows the *ākṛti* of fire from seeing the *ākṛti* (of) 'smoke'" (see text p. 130).

account of which the object becomes manifest. It seems that in language *ākṛti* confirms nothing else than that *śabda* makes manifest the *dṛṣṭa* dimension of reality on the one hand and only points to the *adṛṣṭa* dimension on the other. Hence an overemphasis on *ākṛti* as mediator would ignore the importance of the *autpattika* relation between *śabda* and its object. Thus the presence of *ākṛti* is always brought about by the relation of *śabda* and reality itself. It is difficult to maintain that Śabara would have to attribute a mediating function only to the proper object, *ākṛti*, at the exclusion of *śabda*. Any reference to mediation in making manifest an object will have to take into account the relation of both *śabda* and *ākṛti*.

According to Śabara, *śabda* and *ākṛti* with regard to origin and function are and remain coexistent. There can be no idealistic explanation involved and all illusion connected with the *śabda/ākṛti* relation is a result of human (mental) defect. Nonetheless *śabda* and *ākṛti* maintain their revealing and indicating function on account of which the visible and the invisible becomes present each in its own particular way. Moreover, because of this function it becomes evident that *śabda* is never apart from reality as a whole of which it is in fact a 'part'. Besides, the permanence of the *śabda/ākṛti* relation does not seem to confirm *prima facie* any absolute eternity involved in the relation.

However, Śābara Bhāṣya 1.1.19 which refers to *ākṛti* with regard to class (*jāti*) and individual (*vyakti*) characterizes the word 'cow' (*gośabda*) as *nitya*.[51] It seems that the *ākṛti/śabda* relation is at stake if *śabda* itself is not permanent or eternal. It is relevant in this context to consider carefully Bhāṣya 1.1.5 which is especially concerned with the nature of *śabda* with reference to the word 'cow' (*gośabda*) in order to show the significance of a permanent or eternal characteristic of *śabda*. The significant question and answer of the passage is :

"When one says 'gauḥ' (cow) what is *śabda* ?
'G, au, ḥ, says the revered Upavarṣa."[52]

---

51. cf. Serial No. 35: Śā. Bhā. 1.1.19.
52. Śā. Bhā. 1.1.5 (see text p. 130).

It is important to note that the phonemes are stressed, because there is no cognition of the object without the presence of phonemes with regard to *śabda*.[53] Moreover, according to Śabara, the cognition of the object depends on the perception of the whole arrangement of the phonemes,[54] which are actually the reason for the cognition of the object.[55] Hence Śabara concludes with regard to the term 'cow' (*gośabda*) :

> "One does not perceive a word *gauḥ* which is different from the phoneme 'g etc.', as one does not see the difference and one sees the non-difference. The phonemes 'g etc.' are really perceived. Consequently the word (*pada*) beginning with 'g' and ending with the visarga, namely *gauḥ*, (cow) are phonemes. There is nothing which is apart from these (phonemes) and is called word (*pada*)."[56]

The word 'cow' (*gośabda*) is comprehended as a specific set of phonemes which is exclusively *śabda* in that it does not constitute any other entity apart from the entity of *śabda*. The phonemes are fundamental to any cognition through language, as cognition rests on the actual presence of phonemes. In fact, it is only the specific set of phonemes which gives access to knowledge of the object referred to by the *śabda*, even if Śabara replaces *śabda* by the term *pada* (word). Śabara refers to grammatically relevant distinctions, for example the one between word and phonemes, when they support his view of *śabda* or when he is compelled by his opponent to consider any specific reference. He often freely uses terms like *akṣara*, °*kāra*, *varṇa*, *śabda* and *pada* within the same context.[57]

---

53. Śā. Bhā. 1.1.5: "The phonemes are not the reason of a secondary sense, because the (cognition) is present on account of their presence and absent on account of their absence" (see text p. 130).

54. Śā. Bhā. 1.1.5: "There is no fault, if one says that the last letter, supported by the arrangement which occurs through the previous phonemes, makes known (the object)" (see text p. 130).

55. Śā. Bhā. 1.1.5: "On account of the phonemes there is an arrangement and because of the arrangement there is the cognition of the object. Hence the phonemes are the reason for the cognition of the object" (see text p. 130).

56. Śā. Bhā. 1.1.5 (see text p. 130).

57. Cf. Serial No. 56: Śā. Bhā. 1.1.5 (see text p. 130).

The extent of Śabara's primary concern with *śabda* can be illustrated with reference to the ancient problem of 'modification of phonemes' which was relevant to the grammarians. Although *sūtra* 1.1.16 says, "it is another phoneme, not a modification,"[58] Śabara comments that "the 'y' is another *śabda* as the 'i'."[59] In spite of the fact that the *sūtra* raises the problem of *varṇa*, Śabara speaks here of another *śabda*. The same concern with *śabda* is expressed in his comment on 'similarity' (*sādṛśya*) of words. If *śabda* would rely on similarity, one runs the risk of being mistaken, as for example the term *mālā* (garland) could be understood as *śālā* (house).[60] In other words, if the arrangement of phonemes is changed or disrupted, it does not form the *śabda* or one might be mistaken as regards the intended object of the word.

Actually the correct set of phonemes distinguishes *śabda* as being the proper word (*sādhuśabda*) from any corrupted form (*apabhraṃśa*) of it. *Gāvī*, *gonī*, *gopotalikā* are considered to be corrupted forms of the correct word *gauḥ* (cow).[61] Śabara does not deny the possibility of correct cognition of an intended object in spite of the use of a corrupted form of the *śabda*. This may be possible, because of a basically phonetic resemblance between the correct *śabda* (*sādhuśabda*) and the corrupted form of it (*apabhraṃśa*).[62] Certainty of correct cognition of the (intended) object is possible only through the proper use of *śabda*. The correct word has been handed down through generations without any interruption and this may not be the case as far as corrupted words are concerned.[63] The pronouncing

58. Mī. sū. 1.1.16 (see text p. 141).
59. Śā. Bhā. 1.1.16 (see text p. 141).
60. Śā. Bhā. 1.1.18 (see text p. 141).
61. Cf. Śā. Bhā. 1.1.18 1.3.24, 26. (see text p. 141).
62. Śā. Bhā. 1.3.29 (see text p. 141).
63. Cf. Śā. Bhā. 1.3.24: "Now is there only one word (namely *gośabda*) which has an uninterrupted tradition and expresses the object? Are the others corrupted forms? Or are all (of them) without beginning'? -We (Śabara's opponent) say: 'All of them are...all are correct (*sādhvaḥ*)'..." (see text p. 141).

This view is objected by Śabara in Śā. Bhā. 1.3.25: "...hence *gāvī* etc. may be the result of a fault and have not necessarily an unbroken tradition". (see text p. 142).

of a corrupted word is actually a sign of the incapacity of the speaker to use the correct word.[64] Thus Śabara concludes that "there is among those (above quoted words) only one which is without beginning (*anādi*), the others are corrupted."[65] Moreover, he makes it clear that corrupted words are not the same as synonyms of an object, for example '*hasta*', '*kara*', '*pāṇi* all of which refer to hand. "It is known from teaching that the relation with the object of those (words) is beginningless (*anādi*)."[66] It may be said that synonyms, unlike corrupted words, have an unbroken tradition of their own.[67]

For Śabara only the correct use and perception of *śabda* seem to be of great importance. The specific set of phonemes, i.e. *śabda*, forms the base for any linguistically valid perception and demonstrates the permanent use of *śabda*. It is significant to note that the phonemes are never explicitly called *nitya*. Even Bhāṣya 1.1.16 which says "*śabdāntaram ikārād yakāraḥ*" scarcely throws any light on this problem, as Śabara clearly avoids the problem of modification of phonemes by not stressing the *varṇa* at all. In fact in this context the 'y' itself is not a *śabda*, but belongs to another *śabda* as does the 'i'. In other words, a single phoneme of a specific set of phonemes which make up a *śabda* cannot be said to be a *śabda* itself—it would

---

R.C. PANDEYA remarks: "There were other languages also that were current at that time. But Samskrit was nearest to the Vedic language and thus its use in rituals was permitted. The use of other languages spoken by the people was not allowed during the religious ceremony. These other languages were called apabhraṃśa because they were fallen languages. They could not answer to the norm set up by the convention. Samskrit was, therefore, regarded as the standard language to be used during religious performances and it was therefore called as sādhu (standard) language" (*Problem*, p. 13).

64. Cf. Śā. Bhā. 1.3.28 (see text p. 142).

65. Śā. Bhā. 1.3.26 (see text p. 142).

66. Śā. Bhā. 1.3.26 (see text p. 142).

67. K.K. RAJA comments: "The problem of synonyms is not very great; for, according to the Indian writers, exact synonyms are rare (3), and there will be shades of difference in the meanings of the so-called synonyms. Popular new forms of old words are taken to be their corruptions (*apabhraṃśa*) still certain well-known synonyms had to be accepted".(FN 3: "like *hasta*, *pāṇi* and *kara* for the hand...") (RAJA, K.K., *Theories*, p. 33).

be either a corrupted form of the same *śabda* or it would form an entirely different *śabda*. The reason for this is that *śabda* is always without parts[68] and characterised by *aikarūpya*.[69] It seems to be futile to attempt to trace any explanation of the unchangeable eternal phonemes in the tenets of the early Mīmāṃsā as presented in Śābara Bhāṣya. Śabara himself has not paid any special attention to the unchangeable or absolute eternity of phonemes which belongs to the specific insight of Kumārila Bhaṭṭa.[70] Nonetheless, it is pertinent to our discussion of the relation between phonemes and *śabda* that Śabara speaks of *śabda* (and rarely *pada*) as *sādhuśabda* only on account of its specific set af phonemes. Furthermore *śabda* is said to be *anādi* (without beginning), because one cannot trace any interruption in the permanent use of *śabda*. There is no beginning as mentioned in Bhāṣya 1.1.5 as regards the non-conventional relation between *śabda* and its object.[71] The close association of the two passages referring to the beginningless character of *sādhuśabda* (1.3.26) and of the *apauruṣeya* character of the object/*śabda* relation (1.1.5) with reference to an uninterrupted tradition strongly suggests that Śabara is not primarily concerned with phonemes insofar as they support or establish the eternity of *śabda*. Moreover, it is evident that Śabara's emphasis is placed on the significance of phonemes for the cognition of the object and the explanation of the permanent use of *śabda* with regard to language. If the specific set of phonemes of a *śabda* is disturbed then the object to which the *śabda* refers may be misconstrued and also the permanent use of *śabda* is maintained only by retaining the specific set of phonemes of the particular *śabda*. Further the theory of *śabda* is inevitably related to perception through the

---

68. Cf. Śā. Bhā. 1.1.17: "*śabda* has no parts (*niravayavo hi śabdaḥ*) as it is known by the fact that we cannot perceive a division of parts and as it (namely *śabda*) is without parts, no (variable) extension of it is possible" (see text p. 142).

69. Cf. Śā. Bhā. 1.1.15 (see text p. 142).

70. cf. Kumārila's *Ślokavārttika*: *ākṛtivāda* 5-7 and *śabdanityatādhikaraṇa* 290-301 (see text pp. 142-143).

71. Śā. Bhā. 1.1.5 mentions the uninterrupted tradition through generations: "There is no beginning (*nāsty ādir iti*). cf. above pp. 46-47.

specific set of phonemes of the *śabda* and is meaningfully based on the grouping or arrangement of the phonemes. *Śabda* as a signifying unit is based not only on the concrete support through *ākṛti* in reality,[72] but also through the specific set of phonemes which is thereby directly related to the real object.

4. *Nityatva, aikarūpya, niravayavatva Characteristics*

There is no doubt that *nityatva* (*nityatā*) which in Sanskrit connotes a sense of 'perpetuity', 'continuance' and 'eternity' is a key-term of Śābara Bhāṣya 1.1.6-23. When in these passages Śabara affirms that *śabda* is *nitya*, he speaks with an authority which suggests that his main argument for *nityatva* has already been established and accepted. This is evident in Bhāṣya 1.1.12 :

> "When we can speak of the permanence of *śabda* for a clear reason, then as a consequence of the notion (that *śabda* is) *nitya* there will be (the conclusion) that it is manifested by the effort (of pronouncing it)."[73]

In fact the specific set of phonemes (*sādhuśabda*) is linked in this context of *nityatva* with the consistent use of these phonemes as *śabda* (i.e. neither *pada nor varṇa*). Consequently (*śabda* itself features as a consistent and signifying unit. *Śabda* can be pronounced several times and at various places and is permanently understood as the same *śabda* because of this unifying significance. This has already been pointed out by Śabara in the explanation of *ākṛti* which conforms to the *nitya*-character of *śabda*.

The relation between *śabda* and its proper object is presented in the perspective of *śabda* as a consistent and signifying unit.[74] The coexistence of *śabda* and its proper object suggests that *ākṛti* itself has the same value as attributed to *śabda* which is characterised as *nitya*. If this is not the case, then one has to deny that there is an *autpattika* relation between *śabda* and

---

72. cf. above pp. 48-55.
73. Śā. Bhā. 1.1.12 (see text p. 143) cf. Śā. Bhā. 1.1.13 (see text p. 144).
74. cf. Serial No. 35 (p. 48): Śā. Bhā. 1.1.19.

ākṛti. In fact *ākṛti* itself is never called *nitya* which is perhaps due to the fact that *ākṛti* is not characterised by *aikarūpya* as is the case with *śabda*.[75] A problem arises, consequently, with regard to the status of *śabda* in the *autpattika/nitya* relation between *śabda* and *ākṛti*. One may raise serious doubts as to whether Śabara himself spoke of *nityatva* in the sense of an absolute eternity of *śabda*, i.e. in the same sense as Kumārila Bhaṭṭa uses it, or in the sense in which it is used by any metaphysical system within Indian philosophy. The problem may be overcome in the context of Śabara's presentation of the *śabda/ākṛti* relation with regard to *nitya* by suggesting that *nitya* be considered not as eternal but as connoting a sense of permanence, consistency and continuity.[76] Only in this sense can Śabara's view of *ākṛti* in its *autpattika* relation with *śabda* be maintained consistently and even conforms with his view of the perceptibility of signifying units (*ākṛti*).

The most important Bhāṣya with regard to *nityatva* seems to be 1.1.20 which leaves no doubt about Śabara's view of *śabda* :

> "One says the word 'cow' has been pronounced eight times and (one does) not (say) there are eight words 'cow'. What, if it is so? Such a way of speech shows that one recognizes (*śabda*). We will recognize it, as long as there is no weakness in our sense organs and in fact others understand it as well that it is so (the same). Those, who recognize, recognize like ourselves and are even prepared to say it is not different . . . and there is neither a perception nor another *pramāṇa* which supports that this (*śabda*) is different."[77]

It is important to note that Śabara's argument is based on perception, e.g. when he says that if *śabda* is pronounced eight

75. cf. below pp. 64-65.

76. D.S. RUEGG remarks "...that the linguistic theory comparable with *nitya* will be comprehended more easily, if one translates the term *nitya* by 'invariable' (and *nityatva* by 'invariability') instead of 'permanent'.". (RUEGG, D.S., *Contributions à l'histoire de la philosophie linguistique indienne*, Paris, 1959, p. 56.

77. Śā. Bhā. 1.1.20 (see text p. 144).

times it is recognized as the same by everybody. Perception alone is his justification for pointing out that *śabda* is *nitya*.[78] He can refer to the 'sameness' of the phonemes at the very instant of perception with regard to *śabda*, as they are not apart from *śabda*; the resonance (*nāda*), however is evanescent. A noticeable difference between *śabda* on the one hand and action/cognition (*buddhikarmaṇī*) on the other hand is evident with regard to *nityatva* in the fact of perception. Although there is a successive character of action and cognition, they do not provide any perceptible ground for their recognition as being the same one at the very moment of perception, as BIARDEAU reminds us.[79] For Śabara direct perception of the phonemes is the indicator of consistency with regard to *śabda*. One cannot perceive cognition and action themselves as permanently referring to any concrete object as does *śabda* to its specific set of phonemes. This distinction shows that one can hardly overestimate in Śābara Bhāṣya the significance of perception with regard to *nityatva*. This is obvious, further, in Śabara's reply to the opponent :

> "The *śabda* which has been spoken out yesterday and the one of today is different.
> No. It has not perished, because we perceive it again. In fact one does not suppose that something which had been seen for some time directly and then has not been seen has perished, when one recognizes it while it is perceived again. If one would suppose so, then one would not believe (to see) his mother, wife or father seeing them a second time. One does not suppose necessarily that a thing perished, just because one does not perceive it anymore. If there is no *pramāṇa* known, we know it does not exist. If there is perception as a *pramāṇa*, it cannot be without *pramāṇa*. It does exist, if it is perceived again without error. There is no non-existence. If the non-existence is not proved, there is no error. The non-existence is not proved. Hence as no error is proved, there is no non-existence."[80]

78. cf. Śā. Bhā. 1.1.20 (see text p. 144).
79. BIARDEAU, M., *Théorie*, pp. 187-188.
80. Śā. Bhā. 1.1.20 (see text p. 144).

Śabara's very illustrative argument shows the importance of perception which is necessary for the validity of his explanation of language with regard to *śabda*. One gets the impression that Śabara's explanation of *śabda* neither belongs to nor forms any absolute doctrine of the eternity of *śabda*. His explanation is a response to his experience of *śabda* as perceived in language and the Bhāṣya 1.1.20 concludes with the remark that "because of this it is *nitya*" (*tasmānnitya*). However, it may be said that this statement is not the gist of the entire *sūtra*. The crux of the *sūtra* is his unambiguous assertion that "perception supports that it is 'this' (i.e. the same, *sa iti pratyakṣaḥ*). The explanation leading to this key statement leaves no doubt as to its being the cardinal point of his view of *śabda* :

> "It is so" (i.e. the same *sa evāyam iti*)...
>
> "It is not another" (i.e. different. *nānya iti*) . . .
>
> "No, it (*śabda*) has not perished, we perceived it again" (*naiṣa vinaṣṭaḥ/yata enaṃ punar upalabhāmahe*) . . .
>
> "There is no end of *śabda* and no destruction perceived" (*na ca śabdasyānto na ca kṣayo lakṣyate*).

These clear-cut and precise statements do not give any evidence of *śabda* as an absolute eternity. They make it evident, however, that *śabda* with reference to *nityatva* is within time and perception. For Śabara *nityatva* of *śabda* is present only in the way it is perceived in and as *śabda* and thereby recognized as the same. It seems difficult to maintain that Śabara's view of *nityatva* connotes a sense of eternity in any metaphysical or transcendental sense. *Nityatva* does not seem to be based on any ground other than perception which conforms with Śabara's view that "what cannot be spoken of (as an object of perception) cannot be the object of perception.[81] Perception cannot establish *nitya* in the sense of being beginninglessly eternal (*anādinitya*), or unchangeably eternal (*kūṭasthanitya*). Consequently, it is through perception, that Śabara asserts that *śabda* cannot be said to be *nitya* in any metaphysical sense. *Nitya* refers to the

81. Śā. Bhā. 1.1.5 (see text p. 130).

use of *śabda* only in the sense of being perceptibly permanent and consistent.

Moreover, there is no indication in the text that Śabara has *inferred nitya* from perception. His statement, "no end and destruction of *śabda*" cannot be transformed into a mere projection into the future which connotes eternity in the sense of being without end. The statement is linked with previous concrete experience, namely that *śabda* has always been perceptibly the same. BIARDEAU's conclusion with regard to the eternity of the word can only be emphasised in this context of an ontological and epistemological consistency :

> "With all rigour it seems to us that Śabara has shown in this way only one thing, the continuity of *śabda* between two enunciations and not its eternity."[82]

Śabara is compelled to refer to *śabda* as being *nitya* on account of the experience of a continuous and consistent use of *śabda*. The inability to trace the origin and the end of the use of *śabda* is his support for the claim based on experience that *śabda* is the same. *Śabda* complies or functions in accordance with its proper object in a way that has been permanently and perceptibly maintained through generations in an unbroken tradition. In keeping with the text of Śābara Bhāṣya it seems that with reference to *nitya* only the consistent and permanent use of *śabda* is conveyed. Hence, *nityaḥ śabdaḥ* characterises this consistency and permanence and it is the utmost which may be said with regard to the essence of *śabda* as *nitya*.

Of course, Śabara does not speak of *nityatva* only with reference to temporality. In order to understand better the notion of *nityatva* so that the term may not be misconstrued with reference to the text, it is necessary to see the difference which exists according to Śabara between the consistency of *śabda* and *artha* (which is characterised by *ākāra*[83]), i.e., the difference between *śabda* and the individual object related to *ākṛti*. The significance of *aikarūpya* (unity of form) and

82. BIARDEAU, M., *Théorie*, pp. 187-188.
83. cf. above p. 14).

niravayava (without parts) with reference to *śabda* has to be considered very carefully in this context, since unity and indivisibility often indicate eternity in the Indian context of *nityatva* and especially in the context of *ākāśa* (ether, air). Śabara's emphasis that *śabda* is characterised by *aikarūpya* and as being *niravayava* is a rejection of the opponent's view that the *nityatva* of *śabda* is on account of *ākāśa* and *vāyu* (air).[84]

Śabara explicitly affirms only the *unity of form* of the same *śabda* in the context of *ākāśa* but he does not rely on *ākāśa* itself with regard to the unity and *nityatva* of *śabda*. *Śabda* which is located in *ākāśa* is the same even if it is perceived to be located in different places.[85] The emphasis is on the significance of *aikarūpya* for the immediate and instantaneous perception of *śabda*. The passage (1. 1. 15) supports and confirms the view of the permanence of *śabda* in its use and gives no textual evidence on the part of Śabara for the suggestion regarding the eternity of *śabda* in the context of *ākāśa*.

With reference to the *nitya* character of *śabda*, Śabara further states that *śabda* is *niravayava* (without parts). The perception of any difference in sound-effects does not in any way indicate a division of *śabda* into parts. No variable extension of *śabda* itself can be perceived, i.e. the *same śabda* is manifested in spite of variation in volume. The perceptible difference in sound/speech effects with reference to *śabda* is a mere indication of the audibility and manifestation of *śabda*. It characterizes the resonance (*nāda*) and not the existence of *śabda* itself. The distinction between *nāda* and *śabda* is important for Śabara, because *nāda* is a conglomeration of various parts or a composite product of material elements like air particles, whilst *śabda* itself remains without parts.[86] The perception of different parts of *śabda* due to any change in the material composition which is perceived would indicate that *śabda* is a transformation of air. This could dissolve the unity and uniformity of *śabda*. The utterance of *śabda* would indicate that the origin and destruction

84. cf. Śā. Bhā. 1.1.13, 15, 17, 22.
85. Śā. Bhā. 1.1.15 (see text p. 144).
86. Serial No. 9 (pp. 40-41); Śā. Bhā. 1.1.17.

are traceable in its use, so that no recognition of the same *śabda* would be possible. In other words, if the opponent's standpoint is to be taken, then for Śabara *śabda* would have an instantaneous existence like resonance (*nāda*). Consequently, one would not perceive the consistency of the signifying unit between two enunciations of the same *śabda* which is given through the same set of phonemes. If *śabda* is composed of parts (i.e. *not niravayava*), it is impossible for Śabara to speak of any *nitya*-characteristic.

There are a few other references, apart from *aikarūpya* and *niravayava* which point to the difference between the consistency of *śabda* on the one hand and the individual object on the other, namely the reference to the mat as a composition of reeds,[87] the woven cloth[88] and the imperceptible air.[89] However, according to Śabara the problem seems to be focused especially in *sūtra* 1. 1. 21 : '*anapekṣatvāt*' — on account of no reference, i.e. 'independent' (G. JHA). Commenting on this Śabara says that one knows the *anityatva*, as soon as one has seen the form of the individual object for example, a piece of new cloth, although one has not seen how it has been previously woven (i.e. composed). He points out that there is no such reason or cause for *śabda* as with a piece of cloth which involves destruction.[90] The indestructibility of *śabda* is not made with specific reference to time in the sense of being (perceived as) produced or destroyed, i.e. *śabda* as a specific set of phonemes is not a composition of (variable) phonemes and is not composed or produced as is a mat (Bhāṣya 1. 1. 16). The statement rather seems to be made with reference to the essential characteristic and nature (*svabhāva*) of *śabda* itself. Although this seems to lead to the conclusion that *śabda* is eternal, one has to bear in mind the suggestion made earlier with textual reference that *śabda* as *nitya* is only permanent and consistent in its use and not eternal. Moreover, it may be recalled that only Kumārila

---

87. Śā. Bhā. 1.1.16 (see text p. 144).Śā. Bhā. 1.1.22 (see text p. 144).
88. Śā. Bhā. 1.1.21 (see text p. 145). Serial No. 87: Śā. Bhā. 1.1.22)
89. cf. Śā. Bhā. 1.1.13, 15 (*apratyakṣasya vāyoḥ*).
90. Serial No. 88: Śā. Bhā. 1.1.22.

Bhaṭṭa, a later Mīmāṃsaka (620-680),[91] has clearly established the eternity of *śabda* in the context of the unchangeable *varṇa*.[92] The reference that *śabda* has neither undergone any change which endangers its unity and sameness nor that it could ever be subject to it (Bhāṣya 1. 1. 21) does in fact support the permanence of *śabda*. Similar comparisons between *śabda* and a produced individual object, especially in Bhāṣya 1. 1. 16 and 21, stress only that Śabara still concentrates on the same *śabda*, which he maintains to be a consequence of his basic insight of the validity of his perception and not a result of any metaphysical speculation. It is difficult to see exactly why Śabara should concentrate specifically on (an absolute) eternity only in Bhāṣya 1. 1. 21, if one does not confuse various later traditional developments with regard to *śabda*. This passage gives support for the view of the permanence of *śabda* in the context of Śābara Bhāṣya itself. In accordance with the conditions of Śabara's rigorous principle of perception, on account of which alone he is able to focus attention on *śabda*, any impermanence of *śabda* in its use is ruled out. This condition may be said to be sufficient for the clarification of *nityatva* according to Śabara. The permanence of *śabda* in its use, to state it positively, belongs to its nature as focused in *apauruṣeya*, i.e. *śabda* is not produced nor made by anyone.[93]

Śabara's entire explanation of *śabda* is a masterly demonstration of the result of the correlation between his view of perception and the use of language. On the basis of strict textual reference there seems to be no evidence that Śabara's aim was to establish the *nityatva* character of *śabda* as an absolute eternity. *Śabda* as a permanent and consistent entity conforms to

91. According to T.R. CHINTAMANI, A Short History of Pūrvamīmāṃsā Literature, Ph. D. thesis, University of Madras, Typescript (quoted by POTTER, K.H., *The Encyclopedia of Indian Philosophies*, Vol. I, Bibliography, Delhi, 1970, p. 76.

92. cf. Serial No. 70: Kumārila's *Ślokavārttika*: *ākṛtivādaḥ* 5-7 and *śabdanityatādhikaraṇa* 290-301 (see text pp. 142-143).

93. K. Kunjunni RAJA comments: "What the Mīmāṃsakas meant by the eternality of words and their meaning was that it is not possible to trace the origin of the relationship to a person (2)". (FN 2: "This is called *pravāha-nityatā*") (in: *Theories*, p. 20).

his principle of perception in order not to interfere with reality and does not seem to contradict a traditional understanding of the Vedas.[94] Hence, to maintain that it is important to Śabara that : a *śabda is autpattika* (coexistent in and through the inborn relation with its proper object), (b) *śabda is nitya* (proper to itself and permanent in its use) and (c) *śabda is apauruṣeya* (not made by anyone), is to pay due respect to the text of Śābara Bhāṣya itself in the Indian tradition. Also, this view does not ignore the scholarship and insight of the later Mīmāṃsakas, who have partly based their own contribution on views prevalent in their time and not elaborated in Śābara Bhāṣya itself. The *aikarūpya* (unity of form) and *niravayava* (without parts) characteristics of *śabda* are relevant for his explanation of the recognition of *śabda* as the same. They implicitly support the three main characteristics stated above. However, the *autpattika*, *nitya* and *apauruṣeya* character of *śabda* are made with reference to the uninterrupted tradition of the use of *śabda* which excludes any authorship, which is above the authority of *śabda* itself. This for Śabara is known from perception and does not contradict *śruti*.

Furthermore, Śabara's aim to investigate *dharma*, which is indicated by the Veda as conducive to the highest good, supports the above view of *śabda*, especially insofar as his main concern is not the eternity of *śabda* but the validity of *śabda* with regard to the Veda. Although this validity has still

---

94. E. FRAUWALLNER comments: "Does it not contradict the belief of the ancient Mīmāṃsā in the eternity of the Veda if we declare the theory of the eternity of sound as rather a new one? By no means at all. For the eternity of the Veda does not necessarily presuppose the eternity of sound. For the concept of the absolute eternity was not the only concept known. Apart from the absolute eternity of the word there was also a view, in the Grammarian schools, that the words are eternal in their usage (*vyavahāranityaḥ*), i.e., that they (the words) from time immemorial continue to live in the use of human language from generation to generation. Thus, we may be obliged to assume only that the same view was held by the older Mīmāṃsā with regard to the eternity of the Veda and, on account of the eternity of sound, there is nothing against the assumption that the theory of its (the Veda's) absolute eternity is a more recent development." (*Mīmāṃsāsūtram* I, 1. 6-23, pp. 119-120).

to be investigated, it may be anticipated here that for Śabara the unquestioned validity of the Veda itself is in conformity with the unbroken tradition of the untampered and unviolated function of *śabda* in the sense of making something known to others.[95] The significance of *śabda* is its function as *darśana*, i.e., as showing and indicating the real and pure correspondence between *śabda* and its proper object within verbal cognition and communication. This natural correspondence is not violated by anyone, if *śabda* is characterised as *autpattika*, *nitya*, *apauruṣeya*, *aikarūpya* and *niravayava*.

95. Śā. Bhā. **1.1.**18 (see text p. 145).

Chapter IV

ŚABARA'S VIEW OF LANGUAGE : ŚABDA IN VEDIC AND NON-VEDIC SPEECH

The Vedas are Śabara's exclusive reliable source for the knowledge of the invisible (*adṛṣṭa*), especially of a) *dharma*, of b) Vedic acts and of c) their realisation and result. Therefore, Śabara pays special attention to Vedic and non-Vedic statements especially śabda and the Veda, while he maintains the characteristics of *śabda* in general :

> "The words in the Veda are the same as those in common speech, equally so their object. —Why ?— (Otherwise) *there would be no injunction of action* (*sūtra*). The injunction of action is only possible, if the words and the objects are the same. If the words were different, their object could not be known."[1]

There is no distinction between a Vedic and a profane, i.e., non-Vedic, word (*śabda*). In other words, there are not two sets of words, on which two different languages could be based. The nature of the word is one and the same, as we cannot perceive any difference which would justify two different types of *śabdas* and objects[2] with reference to the Vedic and the non-Vedic uses. There are no additional characteristics to the ones already discussed with reference to the *śabda* perceived

1. Śā. Bhā. 1.3.30 (see text p. 145).

2. Śabara's reference to the Vedic statement "the cows of the gods move on their backs" concludes: If the words [e.g., *go* (cow)] were different in the Vedas from the common usage, it would be impossible to comprehend '*uttanaḥ*' (on their backs). In other words, one would not grasp this 'characteristic of the cow'. cf. Śā. Bhā. 1.3.30 (see text p. 145).

in the Veda. Consequently it seems at first sight that the significance of any statement, Vedic or non-Vedic, would be the same with regard to *śabda*, in spite of the sharp distinction between the Veda and the *smṛti*. This is the case for Śabara insofar as he is concerned only with meaningful, and not necessarily valid statements.

1. *Meaningful Speech*

For Śabara all statements, Vedic and non-Vedic, are meaningful, because the *vākya* (sentence or group of words) does not have another object than that referred to by each *śabda*. Further Śabara points out that :

> "The words (*padāni*) cease to operate, after they have expressed their own object. Now the objects of the words, as they are known, make known the object of the sentence. ..."[3]

This view is elaborated by referring to qualifying terms, for example, 'white', which are not apart from the object concerned. Therefore, the notion of the particularised or qualified thing is given through its quality. "The cognition of the particularised objects is (constitutes) the object of the sentence."[4] Consequently cognition of the object of the sentence is not possible, if the isolated, particularised object of the word is not known or if the object of the sentence is considered to be distinct from the qualified and qualifying words of the sentence.

> "One who has an idea of whiteness, even when the word has not been uttered, has precisely the idea of a thing which is qualified by white. Consequently the cognition of the words is the very object of the sentence; and the latter has no connection with the group of words" (different from the objects of the words).[5]

After having clarified his view more clearly Śabara says :

"If it is so, one has rejected (the objection :) the exclusion

3. Śā. Bhā. 1.1.25 (see text p. 145).
4. Śā. Bhā. 1.1.25 (see text p. 145).
5. Śā. Bhā. 1.1.25 (see text p. 145)

of others qualities cannot be the object of the word (*śabda*)" (Expressing a quality).[6]

Although in this Bhāṣya, Śabara generally uses the term *pada* (word), the above quotation features the key-term *śabda* in the same context. In the context of Śābara Bhāṣya as a whole, Śabara does not seem to concentrate on the term *pada* itself and it may be said that *śabda* is the key to the object and meaning of the sentence (*vākyārtha*) and, thus, one may add of language itself. Only those combinations of words are considered to be a sentence which produce a meaningful unity of the object which is not apart from *śabdas*, but constituted through *śabdas*. The connection between the object or objects of words forming the object of the sentence as a whole is due to *bhāvanā* which has already been referred to above.[7] To borrow BIARDEAU's statement:

> "...What is always important is that *ākṛti* is never known alone, but is always known with the individual, or the individuals, that structures it... One could say, taken separately that the word denotes all the individuals of the same *ākṛti* (i.e. consequently of the same class), while the sentence has to limit its intrinsic value (*portée*)."[8]

Śabara's maintenance of *śabdas* as the signifying unit of the sentence shows the key-position of *śabda* in meaningful language. Besides Śabara rejects through this explanation the view of the opponent who says :

> "Even if the word (*śabda*) and its relation to the object are *autpattika* and *nitya*, the *dharma* cannot be what is indicated by the Vedic injunction. As the Vedic injunction is a sentence . . . The words themselves are used (in common speech), and their object is *nitya*. But their group itself is never used. Hence, either the object of the group is artificial or illusory. . . ."[9]

---

6. Śā. Bhā. 1.1.25 (see text p. 146).
7. cf. above pp. 31-32.
8. BIARDEAU, M., *Théorie*, p. 195, note 1.
9. Śā. Bhā. 1.1.24 (see text p. 146).

One can hardly overemphasize the significance of *śabda* with regard to language and reality, as according to Śabara the object of meaningful Vedic and non-Vedic statements is constituted through *śabdas*. The possibility of meaningful speech is given only through *śabda* in its valid relation to the object To formulate it rigorously one may say that for Śabara a meaningful sentence is the powerful demonstration of the fact that *śabda* and *ākṛti* are always on the same constitutive level in which one cannot perceive any human influence or interference, whereby the meaningfully manifested object of the sentence is annihilated. Misunderstanding of a sentence may occur on account of the fact that *śabda* is not known in its proper relation to the object as may happen, for example, with persons who are mentally deranged.[10] Misunderstanding does not occur as a result of the sentence itself, i.e. the word arrangement, because of the simple fact that a sentence is already a completely unified group of words. If a group of words does not form a unit in itself, this group of words cannot be said to be a sentence. Strictly speaking, human influence does not interfere with the meaningful function of the sentence in showing or indicating something in accordance with reality. Consequently, although a *sādhu-śabda* or a *vākya* (sentence) can be communicated by men, yet its meaningful function cannot be revoked by any person.[11]

2. *Valid speech*

Since *śabda* does not rely on man in its natural and inherent relation to the object, and also, since *śabda* is the basis of the sentence with regard to its meaningful relation to its object, the significance of Bhāṣya 1.1.18 is evident with regard to the relevance of *śabda* in its relation to language as a whole, when it says :

> "*Śabda* must be *nitya*.—Why ?—It is so, because the object is (meant) for others through showing. To show is to utter. Hence there is an object for others, i.e. to make known the object to somebody else."[12]

10. cf. Śā. Bhā. 1.1.25 (p. 146).

11. cf. *sādhuśabda*, above pp. 57-60. cf. unity of *vākya*, above p. 72. cf. unity of object: *Mī. sū*: 2,1,46 (see text p. 146).

12. Śā. Bhā. 1.1.18 (see text p. 146).

Consequently, man responds to the objects of reality by merely vindicating through language the existing meaningful use of *śabda* in its proper relation to the object. Hence, when one sees the object 'cow', the response to the object is identical with the use of the word 'cow' (*gośabda*) and *vice versa*, i.e., *śabda* and *artha* coexist and their coexistence for Śabara has been maintained in an unbroken tradition, which usage we merely vindicate. Whilst Śabara grants the reality of the object as being identical with the use of its related *śabda*, he emphasizes *śabda* which gives knowledge of its related object. Therefore Śabara says :

> "If the relation (between *śabda* and *artha*) is established by man, one might suspect that there is a cognition which is false. Then it would be a cognition of another (extraneous source). On the other hand if *śabda speaks* (*śabde bruvati*) why should it be false ? Then it is not obtained from another man. '*It speaks*' means '*it makes known*' (*bravīti ity ucyate avabodhayati*); it is the sign/reason (*nimittam*) of the (thing) to be known. Now if on account of *śabda* as the sign/reason it (the object) becomes known by itself, how could one call it a fallacy (and say) : 'it is not so ?"[13]

In this passage Śabara is not concerned with meaningful speech within language, but with the validity of *śabda* (and language as a whole) insofar as it concerns right knowledge. The authority of *śabda* as an authentic valid source of knowledge in meaningful speech is the key-issue, i.e., he considers the relevance of *śabda* as a means of right knowledge. *Śabda* is affirmed in its primordial aspect as a *pramāṇa* because *śabda* is reliable and valid apart from any human influence: it is independent of man (*apauruṣeya*).

Śabda itself speaks, i.e. makes known what can be said without error and mistake. The knowledge which relies fully on *śabda* is valid like any cognition. One has to keep in mind that for Śabara, the inherent validity of any cognition is not affirmed beyond doubt by the principle of verification, but

13. Śā. Bhā. 1.1.5 (see text p. 130).

only through the principle of falsification. In other words, the validity of cognition is not tested by showing positive evidence in support of it, but by the impossibility of falsifying it.

> "If a cognition, when it has really arisen, does not fail (turn into the opposite), then one cannot say of it : 'it is not so', 'how it is known, thus it is not; and how it is not known, thus it is'. There is something in mind and something else in speech. When one speaks thus, something contradictory is comprehended : 'It is' and 'it is not'."[14]

One has to bear in mind that a cognition is inherently valid, because it is based on perception, which is in contact with the perceived object and presupposes the right functioning of the sense organs.

> "For a cognition which has something as an object, while there is a contact with something else, that is no perception ...If after careful examination, no defect is found (in the sense organ and the object), then we think it is not defective, because there is no *pramāṇa* for it (i.e. there is nothing to show any defect). Consequently, a cognition of which the causal means are defective and whereby the cognition arises that it is wrong, is an erroneous cognition, no other."[15]

However, this is especially pointed out with regard to the object of the visible realm of reality, where a direct contact between the sense organs and the object is possible. Nonetheless, the same conditions are to be applied for the cognition of a statement, which is based on *śabda* and presupposes the right functioning of the sense organs[16].

Moreover according of Śabara, *śabda itself speaks*, i.e., it makes known the object without error and mistake, because it has no extraneous source. *Śabda* is in direct contact with the object in and through its *autpattika* relation. Hence the object

---

14. Śā. Bhā. 1.1.5 (see text p. 131).
15. Śā. Bhā. 1.1.5 (see text p. 131).
16. Śā. Bhā. 1.1.25 (see text p. 146).

of cognition is on a level where strictly speaking no defect in the causal means can be discovered, because the relation is *nitya* and *apauruṣeya*. Consequently, if *śabda* speaks, it makes known what can be said in an authentic and authoritative way to anyone whose sense organs are not defective with regard to cognising and recognising *śabda*. Cognition which arises through *śabda* is not erring (*avyatireka*) and "this cognition does not fail (turn into the opposite").[17] Therefore Śabara can say of a statement which is only based on *śabda*, i.e., actually of *śabda* itself, that :

> "It is *pramāṇa*, because it is independent (*anapekṣatvāt*). Therefore there is no need for another cognition or for another man. For that is a cognition by its very nature (*svayaṃpratyaya*)."[18]

The core of Śabara's insight into the above *pramāṇa*-characteristic lies in the fact that *śabda* in its *autpattika* relation to its object is independent, "because of the absence of perception as *pramāṇa* and on account of the precedence (of perception) with regard to the other (*pramāṇas*)."[19]

> *Śabda* "would not be a *pramāṇa*, if there were only five *pramāṇas*. As a matter of fact everything by which a right cognition is obtained is *pramāṇa*. One also cognises correctly through *śabda*. Hence, *śabda* is also a *pramāṇa* equally like perception (*pratyakṣa*)."[20]

If the *autpattika/nitya/apauruṣeya* relation between *śabda* and its object is maintained and no contradiction to this proper

17. Śā. Bhā. 1.1.5 (see text p. 131).
18. Śā. Bhā. 1.1.5 (see text p. 131).
19. Śā. Bhā. 1.1.5 (see text p. 131). This is Śabara's 'definition' of the *pramāṇa* of non-perception (*anupalabdhi*). *Anupalabdhi* is a *pramāṇa*, if no *pramāṇa* is available. According to Śabara the other *pramāṇas* are *pratyakṣa* (perception), *śabda* ('word'), *anumāna* (inference), *upamāna* (comparison), *arthāpatti* (presumption). *Pratyakṣa* is related to the others at some stage of human experience and is therefore precedent. Śabara's insight of *śabda*'s independence to our opinion is due to *anupalabdhi*; no *pramāṇa* is available to falsify it. cf. also the statement on *abhāva*: Śā. Bhā. 1.1.5 (see text p. 131).
20. Śā. Bhā. 1.1.5 (see text p. 131).

relation can be found (i.e. to the characteristics of *śabda*), one can speak of *śabda* in its pure state where it is a *pramāṇa* beyond doubt; there is no defect in *śabda* and its object. Thus this relation is the reason for any knowledge of and through *śabda* which cannot turn out to be wrong. In other words *śabda* speaks, i.e. makes (something) known.

Valid knowledge of *śabda* is obtained through *codanā* (Vedic injunction). *Codanā* as a sentence is not only meaningfully constituted by *śabda*, but has also *no* other extraneous source which could lead to error. This is the basic insight which guides Śabara in his answer to the opponent who says :

> "A *codanā* could speak of an object in a manner which is not in accordance with its nature (something incorrect) like any common speech, (for example), there are fruits on the bank of a river. It can be true or false.
> (Śabara's answer is :) It is to say that it is considered to be a contradiction to say (at the same time) 'it (*codanā*) says' and it says 'falsely'. 'It says' means 'it makes known'; it is the sign/reason for the (thing) to be known. What is present as the reason for a thing to be known is that which makes known . . . it is a contradiction to say 'one knows a thing which does not exist.'"[21]

For Śabara a *codanā* is valid, because it cannot be falsified. In other words, the fact of saying relies only on *śabda* which makes itself known without error and mistake. There is no human influence which endangers this reliance upon *śabda* as *pramāṇa.* A *codanā*—in order never to be falsified as a valid statement—must be true in the sense that its knowledge cannot fail, i.e. cannot be contradicted. This involves according to Śabara, a new experience which excludes a mere remembrance of a previous experience. The experience itself is valid, if it is based on perception which refers to the *dṛṣṭa* dimension of reality. However, mere remembrance is not compatible with

21. Śā. Bhā. 1.1.2 (see text p. 131).

validity. "There is no remembrance of something which has not been seen before"[22] or it is a mere repetition of a statement. A remembrance does not state anything new which according to Śābara Bhāṣya 1.4.4 is essential to a Vedic injunction :

> "The making known of something unknown is said to be a *vidhi* (injunction)."[23]

Codanā cannot be falsified, only if the above conditions are fulfilled and it has actually passed the test of *śabda* as *pramāṇa* in the sense of having no extraneous source leading to error. Hence, a Vedic injunctive statement is *only* constituted through *śabda* and is not only meaningful but also valid. There is no *codanā* where *śabda* does not speak, i.e. makes something known without error.

A Vedic injunction is not a mere remembrance. On the contrary "*codanā* is able to make known (indicate) such an object which is past, present or future, subtle, hidden or remote (or of such a kind), and nothing else, not even a sense organ (can do)."[24]

There is simply no human experience which could falsify the knowledge of a Vedic injunction. A *codanā*, therefore, does not even face the risk of being found false. It is absolutely reliable. The knowledge which can be acquired from any Vedic injunction has not been tampered with by any extrinsic influence and cannot be contradicted. Consequently, it is valid knowledge, because *codanā* is pure *śabda* as a *pramāṇa*. There is no other means of knowing reality in its *adṛṣṭa* dimension than *śabda* as *pramāṇa*, which is certainly accessible in the Vedas.

One may say that according to Śabara *codanā* forms the primordially authoritative section of the entire Vedic literature. Although the object of any Vedic injunctive sentence is yet outside the realm of human experience, it is nonetheless, always recognisable as linked to human action through the injunction

22. Śā. Bhā. 1.1.5 (see text p. 132).
23. Śā. Bhā. 1.4.4 (see text p. 146).
24. Śā. Bhā. 1.1.2 (see text p. 132).

itself. For "one calls injunction (*codanā*) the word (*vacanam*) which incites action."[25] This insight poses on the one hand the problem whether the non-injunctive statements of the Vedas are also reliable in the same way as injunctive ones, i.e. the problem whether these non-injunctive statements are mere human insights and human compositions; but on the other hand it provides the key to Śabara's explanation of the entire Veda as being *apauruṣeya*.

Since some Vedic texts are distinguished from one another by different names of individuals, Śabara's opponent points out that the entire "Vedas belong to recent times as they were composed in modern days."[26] Śabara rejects the allegation that the Vedas even the Vedic injunctions—are of human authorship by reference to "precedence and priority of *śabda*" as explained by him[27]. Also Śabara points especially out that the opponent's presumption is not stringently against the *apauruṣeya* characteristic of the Vedas itself. According to Śabara "there is no presumption (*arthāpatti*), (because) it is possible to give to it (the Vedic texts) the name of somebody who is not the author."[28] He explains that the designation of names to texts is due to "the unique and excellent exposition" by outstanding persons, who because they studied only one recension enjoyed a superior reputation with regard to that section; it is a distinctive proper feature."[29] Besides there is no name of any historical person mentioned in the Vedas. The presupposition of historical names in Vedic texts is a false conclusion on the basis of "a mere similarity of sounds" (*śrutisāmānyamātram*) which are associated with names of persons.[30]

Śabara rules out any idea of a human authorship of the entire Veda. The injunctions are the main issue of the Vedic literature and every statement in it is coherent with a specific injunction. Even such statements as "Trees sat at the sacri-

---

25. Śā. Bhā. 1.1.2 (see text p. 132).
26. Śā. Bhā. 1.1.27 (see text p. 146).
27. Śā. Bhā. 1.1.29 (see text p. 146).
28. Śā. Bhā. 1.1.30 (see text p. 146).
29. Cf. Śā. Bhā. 1.1.30 (see text p. 147).
30. Śā. Bhā. 1.1.31 (see text p. 147).

ficial session" are not absurd (*nānupapanna*). They have a specific aim with regard to the injunction or its object and are far from the incoherence found in the utterance of lunatics and children.[31] Even such non-injunctive statements cannot be cited in support of the (opponent's) view that the Vedas are human compositions. On the contrary non-injunctive sentences are always based on *śabda* through their inherent coherence with their specific injunction. "One sees that they are enjoined for the sake of mutual relation.[32] To borrow the paraphrase of G. JHA : "As a rule we find the sentences occurring in the Veda laid down as mutually connected."[33]

Śabara's remark in the Bhāṣya that "the friendly teaching is in harmony and is well established"[34] conforms with his explanation of the "*pramāṇa* characteristic of the whole Veda."[35] The *pramāṇa* characteristic of the whole Veda rests on the import of the non-injunctive statements only with regard to injunctions, i.e., to *śabda* which is accessible as a *pramāṇa*. The Vedic texts, therefore, can be distinguished into a) injunctions (*codanā*, *vidhi*, *niṣedha*, *pratiṣedha*), b) explanatory proclamations of the object/purpose (*arthavāda*), c) formulae to be recited in the performance of a sacrificial act (*mantra*) and d) names (*nāmadheya*).[36] However, only the first, the injunctions, directly point to the *adṛṣṭa* dimension of reality and indicate the object, for example, *dharma* or *apūrva*, while the other statements form an important part of the injunctions and therefore cannot be dismissed. What is important to note in our context is that all non-injunctive sentences are coherently interwoven with an injunctive statement within the Veda itself. Besides, they support the injunction to which they are related by throwing light on the relevance or performance of the Vedic action as

---

31. Cf. Śā. Bhā. 1.1.32 (see text p. 147).
32. Śā. Bhā. 1.1.32 (see text p. 147).
33. JHA, G., *Śābara-Bhāṣya*, Vol. I, p. 50.
34. Śā. Bhā. 1.1.32 (see text p. 147).
35. Cf. Śā. Bhā. 1.3.1 (see text p. 147).
36. Cf. Śā. Bhā., *adhyāya* I for this classification of the Vedas. According to Śā. Bhā. 2.1.33 the Vedas are distinguished into '*mantras*' and '*brāhmaṇas*'. (see text p. 147).

enjoined in the injunction by *śabda*. The link between injunctive and non-injunctive statements is not always obvious at first sight. Nonetheless, the significance of non-injunctive Vedic statements is based only on their intrinsic relationship to the injunction itself. This is the turning point of Śabara's explanation that the entire Veda is in accordance with *śabda* and *pramāṇa* (which is primarily accessible in the Vedic injunction). Consequently, if the significance of *śabda* is maintained, the Veda according to Śabara cannot be deprived of its *apauruṣeya* characteristic. Śabara's explanation of the *apauruṣeya* characteristic of the entire Veda throws light on the full significance of a Vedic statement (*vedavacana*), when he says :

> "Besides to say that a Vedic statement is false, because it is endowed with the same properties as a human statement, is an inference, while the cognition in a Vedic statement is direct perception (*pratyakṣas tu vedavacane pratyayaḥ*); an inference is no *pramāṇa*, when it contradicts perception."[37]

Śabara emphasizes that there is no human interference with a Vedic statement and *śabda* is the only *pramāṇa*. One cannot contradict any Vedic statement with regard to the cognition of its object by reference to (another) perception. In fact all Vedic statements are relevant only because of their reference to the cognition of an object. The entire Veda is authoritative in this regard, because for Śabara the Veda entails the *pramāṇa* characteristic in all its parts which distinguishes it from all non-Vedic texts.

Thus far, in non-Vedic statements, i.e. in human speech, no one has fulfilled those criteria which give the Veda its relevance as *the* authentic and valid source of the *adṛṣṭa* dimension of reality. Consequently, *authority lies in the Veda*, which has been passed on from age to age in an unbroken tradition, *and not in any person*. One might say that there are individuals or groups who are authorities *within* the Vedic tradition, but never, in a real sense, authorities *over* the tradition of the Veda itself.

There is no guarantee of a real cognition, when one refers to a non-Vedic statement. In other words, *śabda* might

---

37. Śā. Bhā. 1.1.2 (see text p. 132).

not be perceived as *pramāṇa* in common or non-Vedic speech, though it may be part of a tradition or highly estimated like an instruction.

> Moreover "an instruction may proceed from a mental confusion (*vyāmoha*). If there is no mental confusion, it proceeds from the Veda as well. Besides the cognition arising from a human statement is 'this man knows it so', but not 'the object is so' (like that). For some cognition which is based on a statement made by man, indeed, goes astray. But there is no *pramāṇa* for the falsity of Vedic statements."[38]

Hence, an instruction may turn out to be wrong because of an error or defect in the sense organs.[39] Besides, some improper motive may lead to an invalid statement, i.e. one without any authority, in spite of its (mere) traditional value, as Śabara points out with regard to some *smṛti*-rules :

> "Some (priest) out of greed desiring to take a piece of cloth covered the whole (post) of *udumbara*. This is the source of a *smṛti*-rule. Some desiring to be fed took their meal with the sacrificer who had bought the 'little king' (i.e. the *soma*). Some observed *brahmacarya* for 48 years to hide their lack of virility. From this came the *smṛti*-rule (that one should remain a 'student' for 48 years). . . .
> And so are the *smṛti*-rules. 'The piece of cloth at the Vaisarjana Homa is to be taken by the *adhvaryu* priest'. 'They make a gift (of the cloth) of the post. (The opponent) takes it as *pramāṇa*, because they have the same author (as the Veda). (This) *smṛti* is no *pramāṇa*, because it has another foundation (other than *dharma*). Some people have done it out of greed and afterwards it became this *smṛti*. This (namely, that it happened out of greed) is more plausible."[40]

Śabda is *pramāṇa*, only if it cannot be falsified as in the case of a Vedic statement. In fact Śabara insists on the link

38. Śā. Bhā. 1.1.2 (see text p. 132).
39. Cf. Serial No. 10: Śā. Bhā. 1.1.25. Cf. Serial No. 15: Śā. Bhā. 1.1.5.
40. Śā. Bhā. 1.3.4 (see text p. 147).

with the Vedas for any authoritative human statements with regard to the *adṛṣṭa* dimension of reality. Otherwise they cannot be considered as *pramāṇa*. This is the basis of Śabara's view that any human statement is a *pramāṇa*, only if it comes from a trustworthy person who in fact actually vindicates the Veda, i.e. *śabda* itself. Hence *śabda* is accessible as a *pramāṇa* in a human statement, wherein reality reveals itself as it *is*.

> "Insofar as a common statement is concerned it is not incorrect (*avitatha*), if it comes from a trustworthy person or if it is pertaining to an object of sense perception (*indriyaviṣaya*). If it comes from an untrustworthy person or if it is not pertaining to an object of sense perception (*anindriyaviṣaya*), then it has as its source the human mind and is no *pramāṇa*."[41]

If cognition of human speech is based on perception which is in direct contact with the object, such cognition cannot be falsified. Sense perception is in direct contact with the *dṛṣṭa* dimension of reality which includes language and thus also *śabda*. Consequently, any cognition through human language is valid, insofar as it is in accordance with the object, i.e. human speech is not incorrect in its direct reference to a perceptible object. However, there is no direct perception of the *adṛṣṭa* dimension of reality so that cognition by means of human speech could be in direct contact with the object itself. Only *śabda* as *pramāṇa* can directly perceive an object of the *adṛṣṭa* dimension of reality. Any human statement which is in accordance with this *śabdapramāṇa* is an inference, i.e., based on perception and therefore valid. If the relation between the human statement and the relevant Vedic statement is untampered with, then this human statement is authentic and cannot be falsified, i.e., the human statement for Śabara is that of a trustworthy person and is therefore not incorrect. In short, therefore, according to Śabara a human statement is not incorrect, if any human influence does not contradict or interfere with the status of reality in both its *dṛṣṭa* and *adṛṣṭa* dimension.

---

41. Śā. Bhā. 1.1.2 (see text p. 132).

According to Śabara, insofar as the nature of the word (*śabda*) is one and the same in Vedic and non-Vedic statements, there can be only one language. Any sentence is meaningfully constituted only by *śabdas*. *Śabda* is perceived as a *pramāṇa* only in and through the Veda. In Śabara's view, the Veda is pure *śabda* being characterised as *autpattika*, *nitya* and *apauruṣeya*, which is why the Veda is said to be *pramāṇa*. The Veda as *pramāṇa*, insofar as it concerns the *adṛṣṭa* dimension of reality, has equal value as the *pramāṇa* of sense perception, insofar as it pertains to the *dṛṣṭa* dimension of reality. In fact, insight in a Vedic statement is also direct perception[42] according to Śabara.

Both *pramāṇas* are together important and necessary in order to know and experience reality as a whole which forms the entire realm of speech. Consequently, the importance of *śabda* and the Veda can hardly be overemphasized in the context of Śabara's view of language as presenting reality as a whole.

---

42. cf. Serial No. 37: Śā. Bhā. 1.1.2 (see text p. 132).

CHAPTER V

LANGUAGE AS THE CORE OF HERMENEUTICS

While the exposition of the view of reality and language in Śābara Bhāṣya has avoided an explicit hermeneutical perspective, nonetheless, an assessment of the view of language and reality in the work as explicated above reveals an evident significance and contribution to hermeneutics.

1. *The Hermeneutical Concern in Śābara Bhāṣya.*

Śabara's significant contribution to hermeneutics can easily be noticed in the beginning of his Bhāṣya, when he exposes his view of language and reality with a hermeneutical concern :

> "An enquiry into *dharma* is an enquiry for the sake of *dharma*; for it (the enquiry) consists in the desire to know it (*dharma*) (*dharmāya jijñāsā. Sā hi tasya jñātum icchā*).[1]

Although this statement is made by Śabara in the context of the *Mīmāṃsā sūtra* 1.1.1. ("next therefore the enquiry into *dharma*"[2]), it is, however, the basis of his motivation to discuss his own view of language and reality. This starting point may be considered to be of direct relevance for the importance of the methodology of any assessment of Śābara Bhāṣya. Śabara's opponent calls it simply a futile task,[3] while Śabara points out,

> "It is rather significant,[4] because even those who know much

1. Śā. Bhā. 1.1.1
2. Mī. sū. 1.1.1 (see text p. 132).
3. Śā. Bhā. 1.1.1 (see text p. 132).
4. This belongs to the answer according to Umbeka, as E. FRAUWALLNER points out in his edition of *Śabarasvāmī's Bhāṣyam zu den Mīmāṃsā-sūtren I.* 1. 1-5. in: FRAUWALLNER, E., *Materialien*, p. 17, note 5.

have divergent opinions about *dharma*. Some call one thing *dharma* and some another thing. If now a man acts without due consideration by acquiring one (opinion) or another, he might ruin himself and fall into misfortune. *Dharma*, thus, ought to be inquired into, for it brings man to the highest good. This is our thesis."[5]

With these answers Śabara characterizes the problem of our investigation into hermeneutics and language when he points to the fact of divergent views of an object and of the consequent implications. In other words the various opinions on *dharma* have a different impact on people. It is not simply a matter of blindly accepting or rejecting an opinion, but it is a question of knowledge which has its bearing on and its relevance to man.

Moreover, this problem of hermeneutics and language can be noticed easily in the structure of the dialogue(s) in the whole Śābara Bhāṣya, especially with regard to Vedic and non-Vedic textual references. What is maintained by one partner of a dialogue may be unfamiliar or unknown to his listener. On account of this unfamiliarity and ignorance (and perhaps also unacceptability) there is an estrangement with regard to the speech, or textual reference of the dialogue. However, the persistence of the speaker in maintaining his own view, even though it is estranged from the listener (i.e. unfamiliar to him) to some extent, overcomes this estrangement. By persistently maintaining to a reasonable extent his own position, there is a possibility of the listener becoming familiar with the speaker's view and thereby there is the overcoming of the original estrangement with regard to what was said. The strangeness and unfamiliarity of what was said is taken over by the listener. In other words, he acquires, on account of the speaker's persistence, what in fact he originally resisted and this acquisition means accepting, from a new perspective, what at the outset appeared unfamiliar and strange to him, or was even unknown. Where such an acquisition takes place there is the implementation, performance and action of '*understanding*'. Understanding does not necessarily mean the abandonment or fixation of views of

5. Śā. Bhā. 1.1.1 (see text p. 133).

the partners of the dialogue but takes place as a mutual response to and as an assessment of the views expressed by each partner.

It is this constitutive, positive element in the structure of a dialogue which characterizes the hermeneutical problem with regard to reality and language. In fact, this characteristic is disclosed by and in Śabara's starting point; *jijñāsā, sā hi tasya jñātum icchā.* The real significance and contribution for hermeneutics is expressed by this statement of Śabara especially in relation to overcoming the estrangement of dialogue on the basis and implementation of understanding. Śabara's concern, which is hermeneutical insofar as it is concerned with the wish and urge (*icchā*) to know (*jñātum*) an object (*tasya*), namely *dharma*, is expressed by the term *jijñāsā*. Hermeneutics connotes the ideas of estrangement and overcoming it on the basis of understanding. This is, on a closer examination, evident in the term '*jijñāsā*' as expressed in the implied tension between 'to know it' (*tasya jñātum*) and the 'striving' (*icchā*). In other words, 'hermeneutics' is considered to be identical with '*jijñāsā*', i.e., '*jñātum icchā*'. Moreover the essence of hermeneutics as 'understanding' is evident in the meanings of the above terms as expressed and connoted by the root *jñā* : to know, to become acquainted with, to understand, to apprehend, to ascertain, to investigate, to acknowledge, to engage in (*ātmanepada*).[6]

What is of direct relevance in this context for Śabara is the significance of language with regard to understanding what in fact is to be understood. Consequently an investigation into hermeneutics with reference to Śābara Bhāṣya must take into consideration Śabara's view of language and reality as regards its significance for and contribution to hermeneutics.

2. *Language and Reality*

The point at issue at the very outset of Śābara Bhāṣya does not consist in discussing details of the possible interpretations or rules of *jijñāsā*, but in pointing out what touches the very core and importance of hermeneutics : the place of language and reality with regard to *śabda*.

6. MONIER-WILLIAMS, *Dictionary*, p. 425, col. 2.

According to the explanation of *śabda* (*sādhuśabda*) in Śābara Bhāṣya, language seems to be viewed as an operative system of permanent symbols which are signifying units. Though Śabara admits the fact and role of a 'symbol-language' as the product of man's effort in communication, he rejects strongly that the nature of language is bound to any convention.[7] *Śabda* is not based on convention nor subject to human or divine construction. A 'symbol-language' as a human technical system is preceded by *śabda* and consequently by language itself. For instance, the designation of an object as directly referring to some particular object presupposes necessarily language itself on the one hand and a common understanding of it among some people on the other. A 'symbol-language' which is due to convention, based on or characterized by perfect technical signs, for example, 'mathematical symbols' or 'grammatical symbols', is obviously contrary to Śabara's view of the nature of language. Nonetheless, the term 'symbol-language' may be maintained in accordance with Śabara in the sense that words are linguistic signs. They are, as we shall see, multidimensional or polyvalent.[8]

Śabara, consistent with his realism, insists that language is *perceived* in and as symbols. A symbol consists in the correct set of phonemes, i.e. *sādhuśabda*. Thus symbols are signifying units which are in relationship with reality. These signifying units are linguistically analysable terms of human speech. They are the empirically perceptible link of this relationship and are also within the sphere of human experience. Whoever carefully examines the possibility to arrive at the signifying units of speech is driven to the conclusion that the ability to arrive at them presupposes an application of language itself. The perceptible signifying units which are the link between language and reality are themselves arrived at by a linguistic operation. This operation, however, is not on the same level of human experience as with man's ability to invent signifying units. In other words, the analysable units of speech in themselves presuppose a nature of language which is not grounded on human experience. Thus

7. cf., above pp. 45-47.
8. cf. below pp. 104-108.

Śabara's emphasis that the relationship between language and reality is not and cannot be established by anyone is of crucial importance. It is this relationship precisely that is constitutive of language and reality by its very nature. Hence language is not the result of a mere expression of the knowledge or understanding of some particular persons, nor is it the outcome of the impact of ideas or concrete experience which ignores convention. The intrinsic nature of language thus cannot be the product of imagination or concrete experience.

Śabara's way of proceeding vià sense perception to arrive at the nature of language is obvious. Whilst he is untiring in his emphasis on sense perception as the ground of verification and falsification, the senses themselves, however, are subject to the intrinsic *autpattika* relation between language and reality. Inasmuch as language and reality are *autpattika,* and further, inasmuch as the senses share the *autpattika* relation, the sense organs, for Śabara, do not form the basis for the *intrinsic* nature of language, even at the instance of spoken, heard or written language. Nonetheless, the relevance of the sense organs with regard to language lies in their capacity of being in direct contact with reality; they perceive what is revealed as being identical with what is actually sensed. Thus the senses are in fact constitutive for understanding reality through language, but are insufficient for understanding the nature of the essence of language and reality themselves.

Further, the *autpattika* relation is not a mere mental construction or hypothesis, since it is the direct, authentic and original contact without any meditation between the object, understood as such on the one hand and the permanently available *sādhuśabda* in human speech on the other. Insofar as the *sādhuśabda* has come down to us by tradition and has been maintained within the context of life, the *autpattika* relation between *śabda* and *artha* may be said to be the same through tradition. This link is permanently perceptible in tradition and is explained in the outline of *śabda/ākṛti* with regard to the individual and class. The *autpattika* relation is not itself verifiable by sense perception, but is grounded on inference, which for Śabara is in any case directly based on sense perception. Even to talk *about* the *autpattika* relation is to presuppose it. Śabara does not fail to recognize its significance. *Śabda* can be recognized as the same because of the permanence of the perceptible set of phonemes and its consistent root in reality. Thus language and reality which imply each other in concrete experience can be apprehended and known by man.

Further, to ignore the basis of language, namely its union with reality as a whole, runs the risk of misconstruing language as a relational system, that is to be found at random. In fact, it is simply impossible for Śabara to consider language as a mere relational system. True, language is inseparably related to reality, as regards its existence and function. But language has its very foundation and origin in the simultaneous, mutual co-existence with reality itself. This relation is the central point of all insight into the very nature of language itself and no question can lead Śabara beyond this point. For language does not disclose an existence which is independent of its relation with reality. Both language *and* reality give rise to *svayampratyaya*, cognition by its very nature, out of itself.

Obviously, Śabara is concerned here with more than a mere structural correspondence between reality and language. It is here where the work of Śabara becomes most fruitful for hermeneutics. Although Śabara neither uses nor elaborates the word *satyam* (truth), yet in keeping with the tradition of Indian thought, one cannot but say that *satyam* (truth) is revealed in the realization that language and reality are mutually and simultaneously inter-related. Whilst this is Śabara's link with the spirit of the tradition of Indian thinking,[9] the term *satyam* is not to be used without a very significant qualification if its application is not to be misunderstood in the context of Śābara Bhāṣya : *Satyam* is not a concrete substance and thus cannot be investigated empirically which, nonetheless, emerges as the

9. R.C. PANDEYA writes in his epilogue to *The Problem of Meaning in Indian Philosophy*: "The pure Existence manifests itself in the form of words and objects (nāma-rūpa). It is the source of words and objects. Words and objects are the appearances of the Real Existence. Spoken words are related to objects in our conversation because of the Real Existence. The Real is the relation between words and objects and It exists in them" (p. 279).

essence of the outline in the explanation of *śabda* and *artha* in Śābara Bhāṣya. *Satyam* thus seems to feature in the *autpattika* (inborn or intrinsic) relation, in the coexistence of *śabda* and *artha*.. In other words, the totality of language (which is what can be expressed, indicated and understood) may be said simply to be the following : It is the truth (*satyam*) of the knowledge that the presence of *artha*/reality is identical with the presence of *śabda*/language which are in an *autpattika* relation. It is the truth (*satyam*) of the knowledge that reality is identical with (or involved in) *śabda* and *artha* which are in *autpattika* relation. In this knowledge or realization *satyam* reveals itself.

If this is the case, how can *satyam* (truth) be communicated ? In other words, is this communication the exemplary function of language ? Śabara's experience with language shows a propensity for communication to a certain extent. His elaborate enquiry into *dharma* shows the aspect of communication partly in and through the oral and written tradition in which the Vedas and *smṛtis* have been handed down through centuries. Whatever has come down through tradition is not an object as such but in keeping with Śābara Bhāṣya, it may be said to be an experience of communication handed down in and through language. Śabara's explanation of language is within communication itself and he continues this communication in his dialogue through and about language. The question to be asked now is whether or not language functions by its very nature as some kind of a tool for man. For Śabara language is not and cannot be used in communication like an instrument, which by its very nature can be put aside after its use. The well-known persistence in regarding language as a mere medium or tool of communication does not conform with Śabara's view of language at all. The persistence of language as a tool is rather closely linked with the view of the various theories of conventional language. They have brought into currency the attitude towards language, whose function is primarily or exclusively communicative. The concept of language as a mere means for communication reduces and limits the scope of language to a labelling of objects by objectifying the 'communicative' aspect of language, whereby it becomes the handy tool in and for a referential system.

It may be asked further whether in fact the rise of knowledge is due to 'the use of language by man' or due to 'the use of man by language through *śabda*'. In fact according to Śabara, *śabda* speaks primordially, i.e. as a signifying unit, it makes known something (Śā. Bhā. 1.1.5.). Consequently, language itself speaks by its very nature as *śabda.* Man is thus within the realm of language and is specifically addressed to by it. Hence man is challenged by language to respond, i.e. to speak. His speech is the manifestation of *śabda,* of language. If *śabda* is known, *ākṛti* is known, i.e. reality is known in and through both of them. Hence one could say : *reality as language speaks,* i.e. makes itself known. *Reality is presented and not re-presented by language.* This is of central importance for hermeneutics. For the very nature of language is to be seen within the function of showing and indicating, which of course can become communicative. This function of language, to make known something, does not characterize language as a mere instrument or tool.

In considering language and its function with reference to Śābara Bhāṣya, there seems to be evidence of a primordial language to which human language responds. In other words, human language would be nothing else than a response to a primordial language (based and grounded in *śabda*) whereby reality reveals itself. However, to speak of reality as a primordial language has its value and significance only if it is also based on human perceptible language. On this fact rests Śabara's explanation of *śabda* and thus his view of language. According to Śabara one cannot speak of two types of *śabda* within one *sādhuśabda* because it is *aikarūpya* (unity of form) and *niravayava* (without parts). The fact, that a *sādhuśabda* is sometimes available only among *Mlecchas* (Śā. Bhā. 1.3.10) does not lead to the conclusion that there are two sets of languages. As already seen, Śabara emphasizes that one cannot maintain that there are two sets of languages, namely, a sacred Vedic language and a profane non-Vedic language. Moreover, there is no evidence in Śābara Bhāṣya for the possibility of constructing through analysis a primordial language, which is set apart from human language(s). Human language and the so-called primordial language cannot be considered independently with regard to the nature and function of language as a whole. To consider human language and the primordial language as separate entities is to reduce them to mere concepts. Rather they have to be considered as two inseparable aspects of language as a whole in and with the function of revealing and manifesting reality as such.

Human speech is a response to revealing reality through and as language, whereby the same *śabda* is present and manifest as a signifying unit. If man does not interfere with the status of reality by this speech,[10] he is involved in the proper response-ability whereby human speech becomes a valid and not only a meaningful manifestation of language and reality. With this in mind the fundamental function of language, i.e., to show, to indicate, to make known and to present, cannot be reduced to the function of a mere instrument. One may say that the very function of language according to Śābara Bhāṣya will be misunderstood if one does not respect the insight that language and reality as a whole are in fact within the realm of human experience as such.

Language and reality as *a whole* are *satyam*, as other Indian thinkers might explicitly say. This is precisely Śabara's concern. For the origin, the realm and the goal of man's experience, i.e., of all human thought and speech, are necessarily expressed by considering language and reality as *satyam*.

3. *Hermeneutics through Language*

Language and reality are the very core of hermeneutics according to Śabara, that is to say of *jijñāsā*, i.e., *jñātum icchā*. Moreover, language as a facet of human experience deserves special attention because the realm of language has a broader scope than the realm of direct sense perception. Whereas only the *dṛṣṭa* dimension of reality is operative in the latter, both the *dṛṣṭa* and *adṛṣṭa* dimension of reality operate in the former. Thus reality as a whole will always remain in eclipse until *śabda*, i.e. language, prepares man for the proper state of *jijñāsā*. In fact, language is the very foundation of *jijñāsā*, since

10. According to Śabara it seems that man can in fact interfere with the status of reality, as it is evident for instance from Śā. Bhā. 1.3.4 (Serial No. 40, p. 82).

it is the real support of one's understanding. i.e., of what has been understood and of what can be understood. In other words, *jñātum icchā* arises out of the tension between the 'known', and the 'unknown, not yet known',[11] and it may simply be viewed as the wish and urge to know the real status of language and reality, i.e., *satyam*.

Whenever reality is not obvious enough for man, estrangement from and familiarity with the object in question call for *jijñāsā*, so that a new view may emerge. This view, however, is not a mere replacement of the previous ones, but their integration which is the evidence of a new view, which consequently emerges. This integration seems to be possible only if man speaks and listens with the 'right attitude', which is in fact called for by language itself. To understand language means to stand under its spell consciously. Then the implementation of understanding is possible. It will be without fault, if it is the realization of language and reality as one unit, i.e. as a whole. Language shows and indicates reality by its very nature, out of itself, because the relation between language and reality is not subsidiary but constitutive. Language and reality as already seen are *satyam* and *satyam* is in fact what is to be known or understood (*tasya jñatum*). Language is thus the guiding principle for hermeneutics, and there is simply no hermeneutical activity that is set apart from language.

Bearing this in mind, 'the right attitude to listen and to speak' is to 'stand consciously under the spell of language' which is characterized by language and that in itself is constituted through *śabda*. It is this proper disposition of man to attain the very nature (*svabhāva*) of the object itself that is present through *śabda* which can be called hermeneutical awareness. Such an awareness points out that language by its very nature neither objectifies nor subjectifies the status of reality which is presented through *śabda*. Hermeneutical awareness, when authentic, sees language and reality as a whole. For Śabara language

11. cf. N.S.S. RAMAN: "...the need for a hermeneutic arises out of a state of dissatisfaction". (The Language of Myth in Religion, in: *Journal of Dharma*, 2 (1977) 372-381, p. 381).

simply presents what actually *is*. Hermeneutics thus does not, as it should not, manipulate what language presents which ultimately presents the core of the *autpattika* relation between *śabda* and *artha*, *satyam*. Hermeneutics, therefore, ceases to be genuine if it becomes an aid to a mere reproduction of an image or of a mental construction; it rests on *direct* contact with reality. Actually the idea of a conceptual production or reproduction of what goes against the status of reality is according to Śabara already rejected at the first stage of hermeneutics, by hermeneutical awareness.

Moreover, hermeneutics is the constant refusal of a sheer linguistic grasping and establishing of meaning, which are the outcome of considering language as a mere instrument or tool of convenience In fact, hermeneutics sustains the intrinsic function of language, namely to speak, i.e. to make known. It aims thereby, at overcoming the lack of understanding. It overcomes the tension created by a (partial) estrangement or ignorance of the object on the one hand and a familiarity with it on the other, as understanding takes place. Whenever the object, which is presented in and through *śabda*, cannot be 'perceived' as it is indicated or shown, hermeneutics is called for. Hermeneutics is constitutive of understanding itself because it overcomes misunderstanding and ignorance. What has been strained and distorted or perhaps not even entered into one's horizon, attains the status of self-evidence through hermeneutics, which makes it possible for the object to be revealed in the way in which *śabda* speaks or makes known.

According to Śabara, an object is revealed by its *śabda* or by its *rūpa*. The object with regard to its nature, significance and relevance does not attain a 'second existence' on a different level nor does it receive any additional physical or spiritual features through *śabda*. Bhāṣya 1. 1. 20[12] strongly indicates that to *know* something does not involve its simultaneous physical presence. The same mother, wife or father are present either through the specific *śabda* (though physically not manifest) or through their body, specific *rūpa* (though verbally not manifest). If one speaks of one's mother, there is a real presence

12. cf. Serial No. 77 (p. 61) and serial No. 80 (p. 62)

of the mother. Speech as a verbal manifestation of her does not involve directly any physical manifestation of her. And if one sees the mother, the view as an empirical perception of her does not involve directly any verbal manifestation of her. Nonetheless, there is the presence of the *same* mother. Both the *śabda* ('mother') and the *rūpa* (physical form of her) that are perceived have their support in reality, i.e. the mother. Whether one knows the *artha* (object) being present through the word or through the physical form, it does not assume a new physical or spiritual presence. That is to say, one is through language directly involved in that which really *is*, namely, the mother. If the *śabda* is manipulated in the response/speech, then the object fails to be validly present. Hermeneutics, therefore, does not manipulate this presence, but it appreciates the physical and the verbal manifestations as two modes or ways of revealing the same thing, which is *really* present. Hence it neither infers nor imposes a second physical or spiritual existence of the object which *itself* is to be known. The object which is present is not limited by its appearances or manifestations, because for Śabara both of them are real, since *satyam* discloses itself in language and reality. To understand what can be understood is therefore to be in direct contact with the object. It has its basis in the *autpattika*-relationship between *śabda* and *artha* and it will lead to no further estrangement.

The real import of hermeneutics thus is not an assertion of an objectifying or idealizing language—as if language would interfere as an intermediary with the status of reality—but rather is the direct assertion of the object itself. This hermeneutical feature of understanding is neither accidental nor incidental, but intrinsically rooted in the revealing character of language itself. Śabara emphasizes this point in the explanation of language with regard to non-empirical objects i.e., the *adṛṣṭa* dimension of reality.

Śabara abandons all descriptive speech of an object in the *adṛṣṭa* dimension without in fact abandoning the object itself. Though the senses cannot perceive objects in the *adṛṣṭa* dimension of reality, Bhāṣya 10.4.23[13] shows that in hermeneutical

13. cf. Serial No. 52 (pp. 26-27).

awareness one does not suppose the existence of a *devatā* in a mere verbal form or expression. But hermeneutical awareness points to the (inseparable) wholeness of language and reality by indicating the actual *presence* of a *devatā* in its invisible nature. *Śabda* does not function as a mere designating power of something which is in fact apart from *śabda*. Genuine hermeneutics consequently, will not interfere with the status of reality, for example by giving way to certain opinions which presuppose that language does objectify in the sense of making *devatā* an object of the *dṛṣṭa* dimension. In other words, *śabda* is not used as a referential term which might be applied within a philosophical or scientific system, which exactly defines and determines an object (*devatā*). The knowledge of the *presence* of an object through *śabda* is not to be equated with the mere apprehension of a term within a conceptual framework, which is imposed on language. Rather knowledge through *śabda* is the knowledge of the actual object itself, which in the case of *devatā* is the knowledge through *śabda* of an object in the *adṛṣṭa* dimension of reality. Consequently, there is no estrangement in the proper knowledge through *śabda* between the one who knows and the object to be known. This means that *śabda* and the object to which it is related are not alienated. Thus it is important for hermeneutics to note that any description which does not present the object in a way in which it actually is, can be misleading, i.e., it interferes with the status of reality. Further, whatever is based on imagination or on improper motives leads to estrangement in acquiring the actual presence of the object. In fact according to Śabara's view of language, hermeneutics will not suggest, even *per viam negationis*, any attributes of an invisible object.[14] A manner of speech which proceeds to give attributes to an object by qualifying it negatively does not make visible, what in fact for Śabara is invisible. A 'distinctive' feature of an invisible object has no more value than a mere superimposition,

14. Nonetheless, the *nityatva* of *ātman* is pointed out in Śābara Bhāṣya 1.1.5. *per viam negationis*, but Śabara does not in the least seem actually to describe *ātman* which is *adṛṣṭa*. The use of the negative in Śābara Bhāṣya with reference to *ātman* seems to be the only way in which for the opponent the existence of *ātman* can be affirmed.

even when it is denied in the final analysis. No description of the invisible leads to proper knowledge of reality, because any attribute (anthropological, anthropomorphic or *per viam negationis*) interferes with the status of the *adṛṣṭa* dimension.

Hermeneutics as traceable in Śābara Bhāṣya maintains that a pure empirical view that leads to a denial of the *devatā*, i.e., of the *adṛṣṭa* dimension, cannot be maintained. Nor does a pure metaphysical view lead to the affirmation of the presence of the *devatā* beyond language and reality. That is to say, reality in totality cannot be known from a standpoint that is absolutely empirical or absolutely metaphysical. A denial of the invisible dimension, i.e. a restriction to the merely empirically measurable reality, is as fatal as any mental projection into the invisible reality. Hermeneutics, insofar as it is prior to any systematic approach, must see reality both in its *dṛṣṭa* and *adṛṣṭa* dimensions and as being fundamentally rooted in language itself.

The presence of the object itself through language is important for hermeneutics, as already pointed out with regard to the *dṛṣṭa* and *adṛṣṭa* dimensions of reality. This is no less significant for 'understanding' than any view which can be obtained through the *rūpa* of the object which, in fact, is not known with regard to the *adṛṣṭa* dimension of reality.

Śabara owes his hermeneutical importance especially to the fact that he realizes the presense of the object itself *really* and *not ideally* through language. (As it has been pointed out with reference to the *dṛṣṭa* and *adṛṣṭa* dimension of reality, this is no less significant for 'understanding' than any view which can be obtained through the *rūpa* of the object which in fact is not known with regard to the *adṛṣṭa* dimension.) It may be said without exaggeration, that to acquire an object, really and not ideally present, without alienating it from its real status is the main target of hermeneutics. The presence of the object is itself grounded in language and reality. They show and indicate rather the object itself, i.e., its *svabhāva*, to the extent to which it can be understood actually. *Jijñāsā* or hermeneutics, therefore, does not entertain statements allegedly leading towards truth as if they were signposts meant to lead towards what really was, is and can be. Language shows directly what is to be understood.

Hermeneutics is primarily not interested in statements as having a value in themselves *in abstracto*, but rather is directly concerned with *satyam* itself, which is present in and through the statement. Hermeneutics, thus, involves an attitude whereby man does not consider language as a by-product of social convenience and necessity only as a way towards *satyam*. *Satyam* is not split into a meaning here and a being there. Śabara's approach calls for a hermeneutical awareness in which man participates fully and is entirely involved in the realization of *satyam* (truth). Hermeneutics, thus, becomes not a mere intellectual endeavour which can be considered apart or alienated from the individual's involvement in reality and his commitment to what really *is*. Hermeneutics is for Śabara, as indeed it should be, a part of the individual's concrete existence that is constituted by whatever he understands. When the cognition of what is known through hermeneutics cannot be falsified and the knowledge gained by hermeneutics therefore is not denied in the actual performance of one's life, authentic understanding has taken place. That is to say, understanding of language (through hermeneutics) does not stop only on the level of head and heart, but finds its completion on the level of commitment and action. In this way, reality and language as such include and encompass man and receive their significance and realization in a hermeneutical response to life. Hermeneutics, thus, overcomes the alienation between man and the object of both the *dṛṣṭa* and *adṛṣṭa* dimensions of reality.[15]

The relevance of hermeneutics for Śabara is characterized primarily not by the person who makes a written or oral statement, but by what in fact is actually stated. In point of view, Śabara does not seem to distinguish between written and oral speech, insofar as he is concerned with the acquisition of knowledge through language. It is obvious that hermeneutics is fundamental not only to the understanding of oral statements, but also to that of written statements. In the dialogue with the

15. Śā. Bhā. 4.3.15 seems to point out man's alienation with reference to man's desire for happiness and thus pointing to *svarga* wherein the alienation is overcome. Śā. Bhā. 1.1.1 refers to alienation from the Veda through a so-called tradition (cf. below pp. 102-104).

opponent Śabara iterates Vedic and non-Vedic passages in support of his own standpoint.[16] He also quotes the texts in order to show their specific relevance, which means that the texts are not and should not be alienated from our concrete existence. Both oral and written statements are equally significant for hermeneutics, as understanding is not restricted to either of them.

Though Śabara does not seem to pay special attention to literature or to the written form of language, it may be pointed out in this context that the written form may be considered in general to be the 'fixation' of its oral form. A written record of an oral statement at first sight seems to be an exact reproduction of what has been said. Language thus seems to serve as a mere instrument in a written form. However, the speaker or writer of any text of the past is not physically present to enable a reader to observe the actual manifestation of *śabda* through his efforts, for example, of sound, rhythm, intonation, gestures etc. It is important to note for *jijñāsā* or hermeneutics that in fact no reproduction of the actual performance of speech is possible; nor is this in a sense absolutely necessary in the understanding of a written text. Nonetheless, certain features like intonation and accent are presupposed for a proper understanding of a written text. A written text does not give any scope for any arbitrary imulse on the part of a reader of a written text. Moreover, it is free from all contingency and affectivity. It requires an openness which as against any arbitrariness, adjusts itself to what is presented in the text itself. What is to be understood basically rests on the *autpattika* relation between *śabda* and *artha* and not, for example, on an artistic activity which attempts to reproduce the text in its original form. The emphasis thus is not on the attitude and behaviour of its original production, which is obtained in a specific situation. Proper understanding takes place in fact with

16. The sources of these passages have been traced with ample textual reference for example by D.V. GARGE, E. FRAUWALLNER and F. ZANGENBERG (Cf. GARGE, D.V., *Citations* FRAUWALLNER, E., *Materialien* FRAUWALLNER, E., *Mīmāṃsāsūtram* I, 1.6-23; ZANGENBERG, F., *Śabaraḥ*).

due respect to what is proper to the text itself, i.e., to *śabda* and *artha*, and to the reader's familiarity with it. Since a written text offers no explanation apart from what is intrinsic to it, it may be said that the estrangement between the speaker and the listener (as, for example, between Śabara and his opponent) with regard to *śabda* may find its extreme form in a scripture. In other words, on account of this extreme estrangement scriptures demand a hermeneutical activity, whereby the reader adjusts himself to reality as it is manifested in and by *śabda*.

A written text has the authentic and significant function of *śabda*, i.e. to show or to indicate, The presence of the object, namely what is to be understood through *śabda*, has still to be acquired by integrating it into the reader's present situation and experience; the reader invariably is in a completely different environment and he may be in a different socio-linguistic context. In other words, a reader who wants to know a text is faced with the task of relating the text to his own experience and vice versa, which may in fact be the intrinsic challenge of the text itself. In fact, a scripture is not a mere record or a mere collection of thoughts, nor is it a mere piece of literature which has been accidentally left behind by somebody in the past as a museum piece of traditional value. The proper understanding of a text is thus far from a mere polishing up of an (old) idea or the mere restoration of a message which has been stumbled upon. It is not (only) a recapitulation of what has already taken place or an assumption of what is still to take place. It is itself a participation in reality here and now. Thus in hermeneutics man rather participates anew in reality itself. What is to be understood in a text is accessible in a new perspective or dimension, i.e., the reader goes through a process of assimilating and appropriating the message of a text. In other words, what is presented in a text is known without estrangement, as language allows the object to speak of itself.

This view of *jijñāsā* neither contradicts nor abolishes Śabara's view of 'tradition' or the vindication of *śabda* as a *pramāṇa*. *Jijñāsā*, according to Śabara, does not exhaust itself by simply reporting a statement which might be in an ancient language and which may seem to have lost its relevance to present-day life and thus appears to be useless and meaningless. Nor does one lend support to the expression of one's own view if it goes against the proper understanding of a text. Both attitudes would go against *jijñāsā* by ignoring the required 'openness' in man as a primary condition for understanding the object presented through *śabda*. Otherwise its impact may be hindered or distorted by the listener or reader. This means that in order not to distort the meaning of a text one may even be required to go against traditional teaching. A passage in Bhāṣya 1. 1. 1. with reference to tradition (*āmnāya*) may throw some light on this issue, though the passage refers not only to the Vedic texts but to the result of a sacrifice as well. In the context of replying to the opponent's argument with reference to tradition Śabara says :

> "We shall transgress this tradition. For, if we do not transgress it, we would make nonsensical the Veda, which is full of sense. One sees, indeed, that the sense (purpose) of it consists in making known the ritual act (*karman*). And the revered men who are learned in sacrificial lore do not speak of a result as a consequence of a mere reading of it."[17]

According to Śabara the injunction "one who has learnt the Veda should take a bath"[18] (indicating the end of studentship) is distorted by the opponent taking it to be that the student return home from the teacher's house with immediate effect. The opponent's understanding is, in fact, not based on *śabda* on which the authentic tradition is based and which should be maintained. Thus Śabara goes against the tradition which is maintained by the opponent as regards what is to be understood. According to Śabara the injunction cannot be understood to mean an immediate return, because one does not pay sufficient attention to the text itself by ignoring the context. The context is

---

17. Śā. Bhā. 1.1.1. (see text p. 133)

18. Śā. Bhā. 1.1.1 (see text p. 133). Śabara refers in this passage to the Veda, although the text quoted is from Baudhāyanagṛhyasūtram 2.6.1. However, there is a remote possibility that Śabara quotes it from a lost Vedic source.

not merely a larger vague text, but is fundamentally related to what can be understood to be an actual part of it, i.e., intrinsic to the text itself. The injunction according to Śabara is to be understood in the context of the statement "next the enquiry into *dharma*"[19] in connection with an insight into the significance of the Vedas. This understanding is emphasised by Śabara to mean not an immediate termination of one's studentship after learning the Vedas, but rather to dedicating oneself to the enquiry into *dharma*. Thus the discussion illustrates that though the opponent's opinion is traditionally rooted in actual practice, it should not, however, contradict what is revealed by the text itself. In other words, Śabara opposes a so-called tradition which seems to be the impact of a mere vindication of a text but not of its understanding, i.e., of an understanding not grounded in *śabda* itself.

Moreover, the above passage indicates that *jijñāsā* consistently refuses to be involved merely in an intellectual grasp of meaning and a linguistic understanding of a text. The vindication of *śabda* in hermeneutical awareness does not presuppose that what can be seen in a tradition is in principle true. Whilst the emphasis on the presence of the object through *śabda* is extremely important in this context for *jijñāsā* as the core of understanding, understanding itself is not to be reached fully by mere attestation, acknowledgement or ratificiation of an object. The manifestation of an object through *śabda* does not withhold its actual impact on the reader. The crux of understanding is thus strictly speaking not a matter of *possessing* correct interpretations of texts as reflections of reality which thereby alienate knowledge, consequently the reader, from the object to be known, An interpretation it may be said, is not an additional feature of understanding, but is rather within the intrinsic performance of *jijñāsā* itself. Genuine hermeneutics is thus the real response to what *is* and that includes also the response to actual life.

Dharma, for example, can be known only through the indication of *śabda*. Although *dharma* is presented in the unbroken tradition of the Vedas, it is not an object in itself that is handed

---

19. Mī. sū. 1.1.1. (see text p. 133).

over from one generation to the other by the scripture. *Dharma* rather is to be acquired anew at each instance of hermeneutical awareness. This continuous acquisition is itself constitutive of tradition. In other words, tradition seems to be the very act of conveying, or 'giving over to'. To be hermeneutically aware of tradition as presented through language is directly to participate in tradition itself, insofar as the awareness actually responds to the challenge of *śabda* or language. The response, thus, is an understanding which is not exhausted by a mere comprehension of data. The Veda, in fact any text, therefore is not to be considered as a mere reference book. On the contrary, it may be said that any text in a very basic sense has an actualizing effect on the reader, as it has been pointed out by Śabara especially with reference to *codanā* that it (an injunction of a text) incites one to action. Real knowledge, in fact, is only attained, when man's outlook *and* performance (i.e., his very life) are 'shaped' by what is to be understood, e.g., *dharma*. In other words, what is to be understood becomes evident in actual life i.e., man is constitutive of his very understanding. The gulf between what is to be known and the one who knows is overcome in the knowing, wherein no split can be observed between *satyam* (truth) on one hand and language and reality on the other. Direct participation in the dimensions of reality takes place through *śabda* in hermeneutical awareness. This, in fact, is the process of attaining *satyam* which seems to be permanently enjoyed in the state which Śabara calls *svarga* (happiness).

For Śabara the attainment and realization of *satyam* and the consequent enjoyment of *svarga* depend on the knowledge of *dharma* which is given through *śabda*. Yet there seem to be more possibilities of understanding an object than *śabda* actually offers. The various opinions on *dharma* and *svarga* are connected with the problem of the multidimensional or polyvalent *śabda*. '*Dharma*', for example, presents 'the highest good' and 'duty'[20], '*svarga*' may speak of a 'region', '16-year-old girls' or 'happiness'[21] and *śabda* itself was seen variously to mean 'sound',

---

20. cf. above p. 12n.
21. cf. above pp. 21-23.

'word', 'noise, etc.[22] It is the inherent multidimensional meaning of a *sādhuśabda* which still demands further clarification for hermeneutics.

Śabara maintains in this context the characteristics of a *śabda*, though he characterizes *śabda* on account of the *artha* which may be primary, secondary or etymological. How Śabara arrives at this distinction can be seen in many passages[23] and especially in Bhāṣya 3.2.1 when he says :

> "What is known directly from the *śabda* (itself) is the prior or primary *artha* (object/meaning). It is called *mukhya* (primary, at the head), because it is like *mukha* (face, forepart). What (as a) further meaning becomes really intelligible from a recognized *artha* through some relation or the other is *jaghanya* (secondary, hindmost), because it is like *jaghana* (hips and loins, hindmost). It is (also) called *gauṇa* because of its relation to *guṇa*."[24]

This distinction between a primary and a secondary *artha* is the reason for characterizing the *agniśabda* as a *gauṇaśabda*. However when Śabara speaks of the nature of *śabda* itself, he makes it clear that there is only the *agniśabda*, i.e., the one and the same *sādhuśabda*. The hermeneutical problem is clearly pointed out in his illustration in Bhāṣya 1.1.5 :

> "And even if it (the phonemes) would be secondary (*gauṇa*), in order to avoid a *śabda* in a secondary sense, one cannot, because of that, invent an object that is not known by sense perception etc. (i.e., another *pramāṇa*). When one says 'the young fellow is a fire' ('*agnir māṇavaka*') one does not ascertain, just so that the word fire is not in a secondary sense (of brilliance), that 'the young fellow is on fire' (i.e., a fire itself) ('*jvalana eva māṇavaka*')."[25]

---

22. cf. above pp. 39-41.
23. cf. Śā. Bhā. 1.2.10-11.15; 1.2.9-10; 1.4.23-24; 3.2.1; 3.3.14, 16; 6.1.44-52; 6.7.1-2 etc.
24. Śā. Bhā. 3.2.1 (see text p. 148).
25. Śā. Bhā. 1.1.5 (see text p. 133).

One has to keep in mind for hermeneutics that the actual burning fire which is itself perceptible to the sense organs does not have a second (spiritual or physical) existence through and as against the *sādhuśabda*, i.e. *agni*. The presence of the *fire itself* can become manifest with regard to its *svabhāva* in and through the *sādhuśabda* which is therefore called *mukhya*. Moreover, the nature, significance and relevance of the *sādhuśabda*, namely *agni*, is not limited to and by this primary manifestation, because experience shows that in a statement *agni* does not necessarily present the most characteristic feature of an individual object (the *rūpa* of a burning fire itself) which is related to its specific form (*ākṛti*). Whatever sense or meaning can be discovered in *agniśabda*, e.g., brilliance, is intrinsically related to the *ākṛti*, i.e., it has its real support in *agni*, the fire itself. If this meaning (brilliance) belongs really, but not necessarily, to some object other than the fire itself (e.g., boy, sun etc.) and becomes present in and through the *agniśabda*, then the *sādhuśabda*, namely *agni* is called *jaghanyaśabda*. In fact Śabara does not distinguish between *jaghanyaśabda* and *gauṇaśabda*, because both are related to a single specific feature which is common to a certain extent (on account of some relation or the other) to fire itself and the object spoken of. The multidimensional meaning of *agniśabda*, which is always characterised by *aikarūpya*, is evident in the different objects to which it is related, for example, to man, sun, fire etc.[26] Besides, it may be noted that a *śabda* may have more than one primary meaning, for example, on the ground of sense perception *agni* means 'fire' and with reference to the *adṛṣṭa* dimension it means a specific '*devatā*', which cannot be known from the fire itself. Moreover, *agni* in the secondary meaning of 'sacrifice' is related to the primary meaning of *agni* as *devatā*.

---

26. K.K. RAJA points out in this context: "The actual referent of the word has to be taken as different from its normal one, but in some way connected with it, either through similarity or through some other relation. This function of the word, denoting a referent different from its normal and primary one, but somehow related to it, is called *lakṣaṇā*; other terms like *gauṇī*, *vṛtti* and *bhakti* are also used to refer to this secondary significative function of words." (*Theories*, p. 231).

Śabara, in fact, uses all the above mentioned terms in his Bhāṣya.

The procedure in distinguishing what is to be taken as primary or secondary with regard to a *sādhuśabda* and its object may be a complicated one. However, the etymological meaning or the common usage of a *śabda* may be helpful and even decisive for the proper understanding of what is to be taken as primary and what as secondary. Moreover, various *nyāyas* or principles of textual interpretations are applied and formulated in Śābara Bhāṣya in order to facilitate one's correct understanding[27]. However, these considerations, rules and maxims laid down and scattered through the whole Bhāṣya seem to be rather the outcome of an analysis, which is preceded by understanding itself. The *nyāyas* no doubt contribute to the exegesis of the texts, but their mere application can hardly be called hermeneutics. Nonetheless, these *nyāyas* may be considered on the same level as linguistic, grammatical and logical rules in establishing a text and thereby its meaning. Whilst a theoretical support (the *nyāyas*) may stimulate to a certain extent a hermeneutical awareness, its application, however, may be considered to be an integral part of hermeneutical activity itself. In other words, the *nyāyas* in themselves are not sufficient for hermeneutics, insofar as they do not take into account the reader's involvement. Genuine hermeneutics, on the other hand, should take into account not only what is proper to the text itself, but also to the reader's concrete experience in life.

This investigation is concerned primarily with hermeneutics and language and it may be sufficient to note that a *sādhuśabda* according to Śabara presents an object, which has its support in reality itself. The support in reality can be discovered in many ways as regards the *śabda* involved. But it is important, that a secondary meaning, e.g., 'brilliance' of *agniśabda* which is always in relation to the primary 'fire', shines forth through the *agniśabda* itself. If the primary meaning contradicts sense perception, as, for example, in "the young fellow is fire", then *agni* is incompatible with the primary meaning of *agniśabda*.

27. Cf. GARGE, D.V., *Citations*, chapter III, "A Statement of Critical Evaluation of the Principles of Textual Interpretation (Nyāyas) employed by Jaimini and Śabara", pp. 252-265.

Since the multidimensional *artha* is ultimately mutually coexistent with *śabda* in an *autpattika* relation, hermeneutics according to Śabara will insist on the multidimensional or polyvalent *śabda* itself, which presents the object in one or another sense. Any interference in the status of reality by misjudging the presence shown through *śabda* leads to an estrangement between a text and its proper understanding. In other words, by interfering with the status of the dimensions of reality, a meaningful sentence is not properly understood and a statement is deprived of its validity. This may be clear in the example where, as with Śabara's opponent, heaven seems to be mistaken for the (physical) presence of 16-year-old girls, or a region, whereby the *gauṇa* character of happiness, intrinsic to both heaven and girls, is violated. Although the statement "16-year-old girls are heaven" may be meaningful, what is presented in and through *śabda*, however, is not understood. Heaven, which belongs to the *adṛṣṭa* dimension cannot be spoken of and the proper response to heaven could be only silence with regard to its *ākṛti*, its specific form.

Jijñāsā or hermeneutics takes a decisive turn through the proper distinction between what is *dṛṣṭa* and what is *adṛṣṭa.* This cannot be achieved without the proper consideration of the multidimensional or polyvalent meaning of *śabda* which in fact, facilitates the proper understanding of the object to be known in and through *śabda.* Genuine hermeneutics thus is concerned not only with the distinction of the *dṛṣṭa* and *adṛṣṭa* dimensions, but also with the multidimensionality or polyvalence of *śabda* itself and its challenging impact on man. The real object as it presents itself through language and one's concrete experience are of central importance for the proper understanding of what is to be known, namely, the meaning and validity of a word or a text in its significance for life itself.

CHAPTER VI

MAN'S EXPERIENCE WITH LANGUAGE THROUGH HERMENEUTICS

The significance of the view of reality, language and hermeneutics may become more evident by our focussing attention on the position which man occupies in Śabara's inquiry. It is obvious that Śabara consciously or unconsciously gives man a central position, though it does not seem to be explicitly formulated in the Bhāṣya.

Man's action are oriented towards the *dṛṣṭa* and *adṛṣṭa* dimensions of reality, and this reality as a whole exists for the benefit of man. Although the two dimensions are never merged into one another, they nonetheless operate together within man, especially as man exists through *ātman*. They are in fact only accessible through man and, moreover. reality especially in its *adṛṣṭa* dimension seems to be deprived of its very function without man and *vice versa* (this can be seen, as for example, from the function of *devatā*, *svarga* and *apūrva*). However, the consistency and meaning of reality as a whole is neither established by man nor possible without man. Man is within reality which is a challenge to his very life. According to Śabara, there is neither a human nor a divine source which could indicate proper knowledge as regards involvement of man in this reality. What is available to sense perception and language, which encompasses both the *dṛṣṭa* and *adṛṣṭa* dimensions of reality, shows and indicates how man should and could be involved not only in this world, but also in the state to be attained hereafter (i.e. *svarga*). Man's action as a proper response to the challenge of life in both the dimensions of reality is inseparably intertwined with his knowledge of it.

There is no knowledge, which in general is not accessible to man as such and which thus could not influence him.

Nonetheless, man is never set above the sources of his knowledge which are in direct contact with the object of his knowledge. Any interference in this direct contact would annihilate the validity of the source but not its meaning. The characteristics of *śabda* are therefore important not only for the rationale of a theory of language, but also significant for Śabara, because of the actual impact of *śabda* on man's life and destiny. It may be said that in Śabara's view, man masters his life best, if he does not ignore the full import of reality which is present in and through language, i.e., when man really understands what is to be understood. Valid and meaningful speech are thus significant with regard to man who has the capacity and ability of finding out their relevance for his life.

Moreover, man's participation in the realization of *satyam* can be viewed in the proper understanding of speech. Confusion and error in this matter mean estrangement and alienation of man from what is to be known, i.e., from what really is and can be understood. Overcoming through understanding such an estrangement and alienation from the object as such is achieved in man's proper hermeneutical endeavour, because it sustains the function of language to show and to indicate. By recognizing the nature, function and significance of language and by assessing and integrating them, it may be said that language is the core of Śabara's hermeneutical perspective which is constitutive of the life of man.

The philosophical significance of understanding through hermeneutics is not primarily a question of its result for man, but lies within understanding itself and can be referred to as his experience with language through hermeneutics. The acquisition of knowledge as it is focused in the act of understanding indicates the basic structure of experience, namely the 'involvement' in something with which one is not yet familiar. Experience, thereby attempts to respond to that which is not yet known or unknown, by renouncing one's present stand. Whilst this basic structure of experience is retained in understanding, the application of the term is guided by the insight into Śābara Bhāṣya itself. Thus such an experience presupposes both *pratyakṣa* (sense perception) and *śabda* (verbal testimony) which render intelligible the object of experience, namely the presence in and through language of an object in either the *dṛṣṭa* or *adṛṣṭa* dimension of reality. How and why through hermeneutics understanding can be called an 'experience' may be better understood with reference to a few commentators on a *mantra* from the Ṛg Veda 4. 58. 3 which reads :

> "Four are his horns, three his feet, two his heads and seven his hands. Tied with a triple bond the bull roars loudly; a magnificient God has entered into mortals."[1]

According to Śābara Bhāṣya 1. 2. 46

> "The 'four horns' stand for the four *Hotṛ*-priests; the 'three feet' for the three *Savanas* (morning, midday, evening); the 'two heads' stand for the sacrificer and his wife; the 'seven hands' stand for the seven metres; the 'triple bond' refers to the three Vedas that embody the description of the 'Bull' standing for the Sacrifice, as one who brings about the desirable results (*vṛṣabha*); *roravīti*' means 'makes a sound' and the last quarter denotes that human beings are entitled to perform sacrifices" (Translation GARGE.[2]

With particular reference to the above passage and to the Bhāṣya as a whole the *correct* perception of *śabda* in its use is of primary importance, yet it cannot be spoken of as real knowledge, if the multidimensional or polyvalent *śabda* is not understood in accordance with the object as such. Śabara certainly perceived the *śabda* correctly, as for instance *catvāri śṛṅgā* (four are his horns) or *vṛṣabha* ('bull') in its empirical perceptible form. Śabara does not interfere with the validity of the *śabda* by pointing out that he is in direct contact with a correct and authoritative *gauṇaśabda* as a signifying unit. In other words, he points out, for example, that *śṛṅgā* is not to be mistaken as indicating 'horns' in the sense of the actual physical form of the hard, pointed outgrowths on the heads of cattle and some other animals. According to Śabara *śṛṅgā* indicates the presence of *Hotṛ*-priests and *vṛṣabha* indicates

---

1. RV 4.58.3 (see text p. 148).
2. Śā. Bhā. 1.2.46 (see text p. 148).

sacrifice through the word. Is Śabara through his understanding of the mantra without error and estrangement, as pointed out in Śābara Bhāṣya 1.1.5 that cognition in a Vedic statement is direct perception (*pratyakṣas tu vedavacane pratyayaḥ*) ? Does he attain the object(s) through the influence of his partial familiarity with the multidimensional *śabda* and language as such, whilst the application of the *gauṇaśabda* seems to be in accordance with his concrete experience and appreciation of objects ? One may go a step further and suggest that he has no other choice than to take into full account the fact of his bias, i.e., being aware of his predisposition and previous knowledge, in his understanding of the *gauṇaśabda*. In this context it is interesting and important to give GARGE's tabulation (See pp. 113-14) of other interpretations of the Ṛg Veda Verse 4.58.3.[3]

Whilst all the above interpretations are based on the 'correct' perception of the *sādhuśabdas* (as for example *śṛṅgā* and *vṛṣabha* as *gauṇaśabdas*) the *artha* (meaning/object) related to each *sādhuśabda*, however, is understood not only with reference to the text but also with reference to the context of the situation and experience of each interpreter. Whilst *śabda* makes known something, the text does not guarantee man's proper understanding of it. In other words, in spite of the fact that *śabda* offers valid cognition, the understanding of meaningful, and not necessarily valid, speech may arise, as for instance in the above case of *vedavacana* or *śabdapramāṇa*, namely four *Hotṛ*-priests (Śabara), four Vedas (Yāska) or four parts of speech (Patañjali) and sacrifice (Yāska, Śabara), *śabda* (word) (Patañjali) or a specific deity (Sāyaṇa, Kumārila), Thus WILSON concludes his notes on Ṛg Veda 4.58.3 by pointing out how difficult it is to arrive at any valid cognition and intelligible meaning :

"This *Sukta*, which is probably ancient, is a good specimen of Vaidic vagueness, and mystification, and of the straits to

---

3. GARGE, D.V., The Contribution of the Śābara Bhāṣya to Ṛgveda Exegesis; or The Treatment by Śabara of the Ṛgveda-Passages cited in his Bhāṣya. in: *Bulletin of the Deccan College Post-Graduate and Research Institute*, Poona, 3.4, pp. 531-546, p. 536.

	Yāska	*Patañjali*	*Kumārila*	*Sāyaṇa*	
				1	2
Four horns	Four Vedas	Four Parts of Speech : 1. Noun, 2. Verb. 3. Indeclinable, and 4. Preposition	Four parts of a day	Four Vedas	Four quarters.
Three feet	Three *savanas* : (Morning, Noon, and Evening).	Three tenses; Past, Present and Future	Three seasons	Three *savanas* :	Three Vedas : cf. TB. 3. 12. 9. 1.
Two heads	*Prāyanīya* and *Udayanīya* offerings in a Soma-sacrifice.	Two-fold words : Eternal and Non-eternal.	Two half-yearly divisions of a year *Uttarāyaṇa* and *Dakṣiṇāyana*)	*Brahmaudana* and *Pravargya* ceremonies at an *iṣṭi* and Soma sacrifices respectively.	Day and Night.

Seven hands	Seven Metres	Seven cases in grammar	Seven horses of the Sun	Seven Metres	Seven rays of the Sun.
Threefold bound	Described in three Divisions of the Vedas; *Mantra*, *Kalpa* & *Brāhmaṇa*	The three places where sound originates in human body, (breast, throat and head)	Three times of a *savana*	Three divisions of the Vedas : *Mantra*, *Kalpa* and *Brāhmaṇa*	Three regions; Earth, Midregion and Heaven or Three seasons
The Bull	Sacrifice	*Śabda* (word)	The Sun who impels one to offer sacrifice	Agni,	Sūrya causing the thunder

which commentators are put to extract an intelligible meaning from the text."[4]

However, the difference in understanding is due not only to the text, but is also based upon man's effort and context. Actually Śabara suggests this indirectly, when he says that one can arrive at the proper meaning of a *mantra* with the help of the science of etymology, grammar and various commentaries,[5] together with the current meaning of the terms.[6]

Moreover, Bhartṛhari illustrates well how one's context is decisive for a specific familiarity of a *gauṇaśabda*, when he considers this *mantra* in connection with *vyākaraṇa* as a means of attaining *mokṣa*. The metaphysical context of *śabdādvaita* is significant for his understanding of *vṛṣabha*, as for example, when he states :

"It has been said that the Self, which is within the speaker is the word, the great Bull with whom one desires union". (Translation S. IYER).[7]

How tradition plays an important part in determining the meaning of terms in connection with language, as for example with *vṛṣabha*, may be more evident by considering what T. R. V. MURTI says in this context.

"The Brāhmanical tradition stemming from the Veda takes language as of Divine origin (Daivī Vāk), as Spirit descending and embodying itself in phenomena, assuming various guises and disclosing its real nature to the sensitive soul. The wellknown Ṛg Veda verse, '*Catvāri śṛṅgāḥ*' expresses this truth in a poetic form. It symbolises speech as the Bellowing Bull of abundant fecundity, as the Great God descending

4. WILSON, H.H. *Rig-Veda*. Translations and Notes, Vol. III, Poona 1926, p. 379.

5. cf. Śā. Bhā. 1.2.49 (see text p. 148).

6. See above pp. 70-71, 92.

7. VP. 1.122 (-1.130 in the editions of Pt. Charu Deva Shastri and others) (see text p. 148). Cf. IYER, K. A. Subramania, Bhartṛhari on vyākaraṇa as a means of attaining mokṣa, in: *The Adyar Library Bulletin* XXVII, Parts 1-2, May 1964, pp. 112-131 and also IYER, K.A.S., *Bhartṛhari*, pp. 130 ff.

into the sphere of the mortals (*Mahādevo martyām āviveśa*) (7). Patañjali asks : Who is this Great God and answers—Speech itself (*Mahān devaḥ, śabdaḥ*).[8]

However, with reference to the term '*vṛṣabha*' there seems to be no single meaning to facilitate its contemporary understanding. Sangam Lal PANDEY pointing out the various levels of Vedic language says :

> "The *Parakīyā Bhāṣā* means the symbolic language or the use of symbols for the description of spiritual reality. The Ṛg Veda describes a religious fact in this language when it describes an ox with four horns, three feet, two heads, seven hands, and three cords. Obviously, the ox is here a symbol which stands for sacrifice (Yajña). ... symbolic language is the language of imagination which creates its own tools and rules to bring out the structure of the supra-sensible reality."[9]

The various interpretations make it evident that man has not ceased in his efforts to understand properly this well known *mantra*. The efforts illustrate how a metaphysical outlook, together with the contemporary concern (for example of sacrificial rites, problems of language), and the quest for liberation, are as much constitutive for understanding, as that which is to be intrinsically known in accordance with the text itself, pointing out thereby, the importance of *śabda*. It is the attempt

8. MURTI, T.R.V., Comments, p. 324.
FN (7): cf. *catvāri śṛṅgā trayo asya pādā dve śīrṣe sapta hastāso asya. tridhā baddho vṛṣabho roravīti maho devo martyām ā viveśa*. Ṛg-veda, 4/58/3.

See also Patañjali, *Vyākaraṇa-mahābhāṣya* (ed. F. Kielhorn, first edition 1880, third edition, 1962), p. 3.

T.R.V. MURTI may be considered to be a contemporary representative of this ancient Brahmanical tradition who, in this article, gives its significance for today. Cf. also MURTI, T.R.V., Presidential Address on the Indian Philosophical Congress, 37th Session (Chandigarh) 1963. *Some Thoughts on the Indian Philosophy of Language* (Printed by Laksmi Das, B.H.U. Press, Varanasi.)

9. PANDEY, S. L., Indian Views of Theological Statements, in: *Bharata Manisha Quarterly*, 1 (1976) No. 4. 33-41. p. 35.

at proper understanding that *śabda*, e.g., *vṛṣabha* ('bull') is understood differently in different contexts : Yāska, Śabara and in recent research S.L. PANDEY understand it as 'sacrifice', Sāyaṇa and Kumārlia as a deity, Patañjali as '*śabda*' (word), Bhartṛhari as '*śabda*' (-brahman) and among modern interpreters T.R.V. MURTI as *vāk*.

Śabara's insight that *śabdapramāṇa* makes known something without error and mistake, thus significantly points out that man has the *possibility* of acquiring valid knowledge, which cannot be falsified. Such knowledge cannot by itself be controversial because it is *svayaṃpratyaya*. However, because of doubts over the proper understanding of texts on account of the different conditions of the various interpretations, Śabara, as already seen, argues a case in his Bhāṣya that the certainty or validity of knowledge through language only *seems* to be contradicted. The significance of this point is more evident when, in discussing the validity of verbal knowledge, D.M. DATTA says :

> "... *if knowledge ceases to be self-evident, it so far ceases to be knowledge itself*, and it is not the case that when self-evidence ceases to certify knowledge, knowledge is left behind to be certified by some other method. . . . When ten different arguments are adduced to ratify a particular knowledge, what is achieved is not directly the ascertainment of validity (which is congenital with knowledge itself), but the removal of ten actual or possible sources of doubt or contradiction which stand in the way of knowledge itself."[10]

Whilst Śabara argues a case for certainty and validity, proper knowledge itself, however, is in no way altered, though his argument nonetheless, functions as a process of understanding for one who desires proper knowledge.

The above discussion shows that the understanding of a text, according to Śabara, makes very significant man's actual involvement in what is revealed in and through language. If

10. DATTA, D.M., *Ways*. pp. 346-347.

the object to be known is neither affected by one's pre-understanding of it nor could be manipulated with (as for instance, in the case of a lie), there is no interference between *śabda* and *artha* and thus a *sādhuśabda* is perfectly revealed by correct perception, i.e., without hiding or distorting whatever can be understood. That is to say, a particular perception and insight functions as proper knowledge when it is self-evident through language. In an instance where such a perception is denied in the process of man's proper understanding of what is yet to be known, or, if the perception is fundamentally shaken by doubts and contradiction, the validity of such perception is no longer to be maintained. Whilst this process is characterised by man's concrete involvement in what is presented through language, there is now a radical negation involved, in that, what was first improperly perceived is now correctly seen in the process of proper understanding. This process of negation continues until knowledge is proper in accordance with what is revealed in the text itself. Such a negation can only take place because of a radical openness of man towards *śabda* and its object. The denial of a previous familiarity and of being open towards something which is yet unfamiliar or unknown in the process of understanding a text, is in fact based on the nature and function of language. It is such a process of proper understanding that may be said to be an *experience* with language.

The negation is not simply a correction of what may have been a partially wrong understanding of an object. Such a correction would be a contradiction in terms, since understanding is proper only if it is based on *pratyakṣa* (direct perception of the object); in any partial understanding of an object there would be no *pratyakṣa* according to Śabara. Nor can man arrive through negation at a characteristic of an object from previous understanding of it, simply because this understanding has been negated by the change of conditions in the process of understanding. Further the negation is not a mere demarcation of what the object is not; it shows rather a new dimension of the object (and thus, according to Śabara a new object itself), which is not identical with the previous understanding of it. In other words, perception of a *śabda* as a signifying unit in hermeneutical activity contradicts the object as previously seen through the same *śabda*. That is to say what has been believed and thought to be present through *śabda* is not shown by language itself, because there was an extraneous source that interfered with the relation of *śabda* and *artha*, as for example, with one's personal bias and predisposition. Moreover, the new perception cannot be due to a mere remembrance of a past experience; what is new is simply not a reiteration of any perevious knowledge. For Śabara, proper understanding means that something new shines forth through language which has overcome what has been strained and distorted in one's previous outlook. The very act of understanding is in fact a rejection of an apparent evidence in the previous response to *śabda*, whereby the old 'knowledge' itself vanishes as being false. Such understanding is experience through hermeneutics and that is a process which is to reveal the object to be known in its original and authentic dimension. This is to say that the vulnerability of human 'understanding', particularly with referencee to hermeneutics and language, emphasizes what for Śabara is the invulnerability of what actually *is*.

Hermeneutics, strictly speaking, does not create anything new in the object to be understood. Rather it makes man aware of what was originally present and which has not been discovered and acquired by man. Understanding, gained through hermeneutics, remains valid until its validity is annihilated by another experience through the hermeneutical process. The 'openness' intrinsic to hermeneutics cannot be specifically described, yet it is evident in the process of understanding which in some way or the other negates a previous 'understanding'. This openness is the characteristic feature of hermeneutics which means that it is not limited by one's expectations of what is to be understood. Though there seems to be in any hermeneutical activity a tendency to ask 'what it is', the core of hermeneutical activity cannot be 'what it is expected to be' as this would be a mere acknowledgement of what has been already understood. In other words, the same conditions of understanding obtain in the attempt to arrive at an answer to what is to be known. Moreover, the openness implies that anything newly acquired may be lost as well. In all understanding there is the involvement of man's realization of *satyam* through hermeneutics. Though it gives certainty and validity of knowledge, yet it cannot be considered as absolute or ultimate. Man in fact has to be aware that his actual understanding can be falsified without the guarantee of further understanding, i.e., man is not the master of the understanding of language in spite of his inextricable participation; he can only 'prepare' himself for knowledge within the possibility of hermeneutics, i.e. in the process of the proper understanding of language.

Genuine hermeneutics obviously, does not go against the intrinsic validity of *śabda* as *pramāṇa*, but emphasizes the possibility of attaining knowledge of what is to be understood through language. Language, thereby, becomes the core of hermeneutics and is necessarily constitutive of man's life. Hermeneutics is also the realization on the part of man, through language, of the limitations of his understanding. Authentic hermeneutics which always reveals something new, is thus identical not with *smṛti* but with *anubhūti*[11] and is characterised by the process of understanding itself. Hermeneutics is an experience. It is neither static nor a mere passive receptivity of the understanding of a text; it is a dynamic response to what is revealed through *śabda*, i.e., language. Language shows and indicates reality in its totality (i.e., in both dimensions of the *dṛṣṭa* and *adṛṣṭa*), which is known to man through hermeneutics. From a hermeneutical perspective, experience and knowledge do not by themselves imply that man could apprehend them in separation or in sequence, where each has an independent being and meaning, because they are themselves identical insofar as there can be no knowledge without experience and no experience without knowledge.[12]

---

11. D.M. DATTA observes that "The experience which reveals the new (i.e. knowledge proper) is called anubhūti (1), whereas reproduced knowledge is called smṛti (2). Thus novelty comes to be considered an essential quality of knowledge".

"FN I Bhāṣā-paricceda (Kārikāvalī with the com. Siddhāntamuktāvalī, Nirnayasagara, p. 232.

FN 2 Ibid." (DATTA, D.M., *Ways*, p. 23).

12. Though modern psychoanalysis questions the possibility of emotion devoid of cognition it is interesting to note T.R.V. MURTI's observation: "Knowledge is a cognitive experience, and it has to be distinguished

Knowledge as experience for Śabara has its impact on man's concrete existence especially with reference to his philosophical and religious quest to understand what was, is, and can be relevant for his actual life. Such understanding, which in fact, is an experience through hermeneutics, questions the exclusive views from a purely anthropological and theological, empirical and metaphysical standpoint. This is so, because they are abstracted from man's participation and involvement in reality which is revealed through the nature and function of language in both dimensions. Knowledge through hermeneutics is the outcome of a sincere religious and philosophical endeavour to come to grips with a constant positive questioning which cannot presuppose any absolute answers. Proper understanding as an experience through hermeneutics varies in accordance with the context and situation of the one who earnestly desires to know. As the process of understanding takes place through language, language plays a key-role in understanding. Yet the very understanding of language involves hermeneutics. In fact, there is no understanding of language and thus of reality as a whole without hermeneutics. Thus the question "What does it really mean to understand ?" is not answered by reality through "language and hermeneutics", but as initially brought into focus through "hermeneutics and language".

Elements for a theory of hermeneutics as an aid to proper understanding which is basic for any religious and philosophical enquiry have been attempted in this investigation into Śābara Bhāṣya in its various hermeneutical aspects. Understanding, however, fulfils itself only in man's actual hermeneutical endeavour through language, which really participates with his perspective of reality. For Śabara reality itself is a challenge which finds its expression through language and which, further is the

---

from types of non-cognitive experience, such willing and feeling as exemplified by volitional acts or emotional states as pleasure, anger or lust. What is peculiar about the cognitive attitude is that we want to 'see' or 'take in' things as they are, as they obtain in reality; we do not want to add or modify or distort the given, and to the extent we do this, it is not knowledge". (MURTI, T.R.V., Knowledge and Truth, in: R.C. PANDEYA, S.R. BHATT (eds.), *Knowledge, Culture and Value*, Delhi, 1976).

basic issue in his enquiry into *dharma*. Śabara's perspective of what it means to understand and thereby to have knowledge, is still relevant for us today in its implications for life : first, to uphold the function of criticism in the attempt to overcome man's estrangement and alienation by the removal of ignorance, bias and habits which obstruct the process of understanding, and secondly, to attempt, thereby, to make evident the significance of man's constant desire and urge to know (*jijñāsā*) what really is. This is vital because man masters his life best, if he does not ignore the full import of reality which is present in and through language, i.e., when man really understands that which is to be understood, *satyam*.

APPENDIX

TEXTUAL SOURCES IN ROMAN SCRIPT

TEXTUAL SOURCES IN DEVANAGARI SCRIPT

(FW refers to *Mīmāṃsāsūtrabhāṣyam* I, 1, 1-5, edited by E. FRAUWALLNER. The first figure refers to the page and the following to the lines.)

CHAPTER II

1. *Mī. sū.* 1. 1. 2 (FW 16, 8):
codanālakṣaṇo 'rtho dharmaḥ

Śā. Bhā. 1. 1. 2 (FW 16, 11-12):
tayā yo lakṣyate, so 'rthaḥ puruṣaṃ niḥśreyasena saṃyunakti iti pratijānīmahe.

2. *Śā, Bhā.* 1. 1. 5 (FW 30, 7-9):
na ca arthavyapadeśam antareṇa buddhe rūpopalambhanam. tasmān nāvyapadeśyā buddhir, avyapadeśyaṃ ca naḥ pratyakṣam. tasmād apratyakṣā buddhiḥ.

6. *Sā. Bhā.* 1. 1. 5 (FW 28, 17-19):
syād etad evaṃ, yady arthākārā buddhiḥ syāt. nirākārā tu no buddhiḥ, ākāravān bāhyo 'rthaḥ. sa hi bahirdeśasaṃbaddhaḥ pratyakṣam upalabhyate. arthaviṣayā hi pratyakṣabuddhir na buddhyantaraviṣayā.

Śā. Bhā. 1, 1. 5 (FW 30, 12-13):
ṣākāraṃ cārthaṃ pratyakṣam evāvagacchāmaḥ. tasmād arthālambanaḥ pratyayaḥ.

16. *Śā. Bhā.* 1. 1. 5 (FW 60, 21-22):
avināśi vāre 'yam ātmā anucchittidharmā, mātrāsaṃsargas tv asya bhavati.

Śā. Bhā. 1. 1. 5 (FW 58, 23-24):
ataḥ pravṛttyāvagamyate "nūnam asāv anityān avagaccati"

17. *Śā, Bhā.* 1. 1. 5 (FW 60, 6-7):
ayam evābhyupāyo jñātavyānām arthānāṃ "yo yathā jñāyate. ṣa tathā" iti.

18. *Śā. Bhā.* 1. 1. 5 (FW 56, 2):

pratyagātmani caitad bhavati.

19. *Śā. Bhā.* 1. 1. 5 (FW 56, 12-15):

"sa vāre 'yam ātmā" iti prakṛtya āmananti "aśīryo na hi śīryata" iti. tathā "avināśi vāre 'yam ātmā anucchittidharmā" iti. vinaśvaraṃ ca vijñānam. tasmād vinaśvarād anyaḥ sa ity avagacchāmaḥ.

20. *Śā. Bhā.* 1. 1. 5 (FW 58, 11-12)

svayamjyotiṣṭvavacanāt. atrāpi brāhmaṇaṃ bhavati "atrāyaṃ puruṣaḥ svayaṃjyotir bhavati" iti.

21. *Śā. Bhā.* 1. 1. 5 (FW 58, 5-9):

tena sarve svena svenātmanā ātmānam upalabhamānāḥ santy eva, yady api parapuruṣair nopalabhyanta iti. athāsmin arthe brāhmaṇaṃ bhavati "śāntāyāṃ vāci kiṃjyotir evāyaṃ puruṣaḥ ? ātmajyotiḥ, samrāḍ iti hovāca" iti.

22. *Śā. Bhā.* 1. 1. 5 (FW 52, 17; 54, 1-3):

icchayā ātmānam upalabhāmahe. . . . atha vijñānād anyo vijñātā nityas, tata ekasmin ahani ya upalabdhā, aparedyur api sa evaiṣiṣyati. itarathā icchānupapannā syāt.

23. *Śā. Bhā.* 1.1. 5 (FW 60, 6-7)

ataḥ svayam avagamyamānatvād asti tadvyatiriktaḥ puruṣa iti.

24. *Śā. Bhā.* 1. 1. 5 (FW 50, 3-6.8 11-12)

ṣarīrasaṃbandhād, yasya tac charīraṃ, so 'pi tair yajñāyudhair "yajñāyudhī" ity ucyate.

āha; ko 'sāv anyo ? nainam upalabhāmahe. —nanu prāṇādibhir enam upalabhāmahe. . . . na prāṇādayaḥ śarīraguṇāḥ. . . . sukhādayaś ca svayam upalabhyante, na rūpādaya iva śarīraguṇāḥ pareṇāpi. tasmāc charīraguṇavaidharmyād anyaḥ śarīrād yajñāyudhīti.

47. *Śā. Bhā.* 1. 1. 5 (FW 60, 6-7)
ayam evābhyupāyo jñātavyānām arthānāṃ "yo yathā jñāyate, sa tathā" iti.

54. *Śā. Bhā.* 1. 1. 5 (FW 48, 7):
anupalabdhe ca devatādāv arthe 'narthakaṃ saṃjñākaraṇam aśakyaṃ ca.

56. *Śā. Bhā.* 1. 1. 5 (FW 30, 7-9):
tasmān nāvyapadeśyā buddhir, avyapadeśyaṃ ca naḥ pratyakṣam. tasmād apratyakṣā buddhiḥ.

59. *Śā. Bhā.* 1. 1. 5 (FW 40, 14-16):
nanv ākṛtiḥ sādhyāsti vā na veti ?—na pratyakṣā satī sādhyā bhavitum arhati. "rucakaḥ, svastiko, vardhamānaka" iti hi pratyakṣam dṛśyate.

CHAPTER III

1. *Mī. sū.* 1. 1. 2 (FW 16, 8):
codanālakṣaṇo 'rtho dharmaḥ.

2. *Śā. Bhā.* 1. 1. 5 (FW 24, 7):
upadeśo hi bhavati. upadeśa iti viśiṣṭasya śabdasya uccāraṇam.

8. *Śā· Bhā.* 1. 1. 5 (FW 38, 4-5):
śrotragrahaṇe hy arthe loke śabdaśabdaḥ prasiddhaḥ, te ca śrotragrahaṇāḥ.

12. *Śā. Bhā,* 1. 1. 5 (FW 60, 6-7):
ayam evābhyupāyo jñātavyānām arthānāṃ "yo yathā jñāyate, sa tathā" iti.

13. *Śā. Bhā.* 1. 1.5 (FW 30, 18-19):
anumānaṃ jñātasaṃbandhasya ekadeśadarśanād ekadeśāntare 'saṃnikṛṣṭe 'rthe buddhiḥ.

14. *Mī. sū.* 1. 1. 5 (FW 22, 21) :
autpattikas tu śabdasyārthena saṃbandhas . . .

16. *Śā. Bhā.* 1. 1. 5 (FW 24, 3-5) :

autpattika iti nityam brūmaḥ. utpattir hi bhāva ucyate lakṣaṇayā. aviyuktaḥ śabdārthayor bhāvaḥ saṃbandhena, notpannayoḥ paścāt saṃbandhaḥ.

18. *Śā. Bhā.* 1. 1. 5 (FW 34, 15) :

apauruṣeyaḥ śabdasyārthena saṃbandhas . . .
Śā. Bhā. 1. 1. 5 (FW 42, 16-18) :
apauruṣeyatvāt saṃbandhasya siddham iti. —kathaṃ punar idam avagamyate "apauruṣeya eṣa saṃbandha" iti ? —puruṣasya saṃbandhur abhāvāt.—

19. *Śā. Bhā.* 1. 1. 5 (FW 42, 12) :

yat śabde vijñāte 'rtho vijñāyate.

21. *Śā. Bhā.* 1. 1. 5 (FW 42, 16) :

apauruṣeyatvāt saṃbandhasya siddham iti.—

23. *Śā. Bhā.* 1. 1. 5 (FW 44, 4-5) :

saṃpratipattau hi kartṛvyavahartror arthaḥ sidhyati, na vipratipattau.

24. *Śā. Bhā.* 1. 1.5 (FW 44, 9-11) :

na hi vismṛte "vṛddhir ādaij" ity[1] asya sūtrasya kartari "vṛddhir yasyācām ādis, tad vṛddham" iti[2] kiṃcit pratīyeta.

1. Pāṇini I, 1, 1. 2. Pāṇini I, 1, 73.

25. *Śa. Bhā.* 1. 1. 5 (FW 46, 12-14) :

yathā asmin deśe sāsnādimati gośabdaḥ, evaṃ sarveṣu durgameṣv api. bahavaḥ saṃbandhāraḥ kathaṃ saṃgamsyante. eko 'pi na śaknuyāt. ato nāsti saṃbandhā.

27. *Śā Bhā.* 1. 1. 5. (FW 44, 13-14) :

yady api ca vismaraṇam upapadyeta, tathāpi na pramāṇam antareṇa sambandhāraṃ pratipadyemahi, . . .

28. *Śā. Bhā.* 1. 1. 5 (FW 44, 21) :
siddhavad, upadeśāt.

29. *Śā. Bhā.* 1. 1. 5 (FW 46, 2-5) :

vṛddhhānāṃ svārthena vyavaharamānānām upaśṛṇvanto bālāḥ pratyakṣam arthaṃ pratipadyamānā dṛśyante. te 'pi vṛddhā yadā bālā āsaṃs, tadā 'nyebhyo vṛddhebhyas, te 'py anyebhya iti nāsti ādir ity . . .

30. *Śā. Bhā.* 1. 1. 5 (FW 46, 16-48,1) :

na hi saṃbandhavyatiriktaḥ kaścit kālo 'sti, yasmin na kaścid api śabdaḥ kenacid arthena saṃbaddha āsīt. — katham ? — saṃbandhakriyaiva hi nopapadyate. avaśyam anena saṃbandhaṃ kurvatā kenacic chabdena kartavyaḥ. yena kriyeta, tasya kena kṛtaḥ ? athānyena kenacit kṛtaḥ, tasya keneti, tasya keneti naivāvatiṣṭhate. tasmād avaśyam anena saṃbandhaṃ kurvatā akṛtasaṃbandhāḥ kecana śabdā vṛddhavyavahārasiddhā abhyupagantavyāḥ.

32. *Śā. Bhā.* 1. 1. 5 (FW 36, 22-38, 1) :

svabhāvato hy asaṃbaddhāv etau śabdārthau. mukhe hi śabdam upalabhāmahe, bhūmāv artham. "śabdo 'yaṃ na tv arthaḥ, artho 'yaṃ na śabda" iti ca vyapadiśanti. rūpabhedo 'pi bhavati. "gaur" iti imaṃ śabdam uccārayanti, sāsnādimantam artham avabudhyante.

33. *Śā. Bhā.* 1. 1. 5 (FW 40, 13-14) :

atha "gaur" ity asya śabdasya ko 'rthaḥ ? —sāsnādiviśiṣṭā ākṛtir iti brūmaḥ.—

37. *Śā. Bhā.* 1. 1. 5 (FW 40, 14-15) :

nanv ākrtiḥ sādhyāsti vā na veti ? —na pratyakṣā satī sādhyā bhavitum arhati.

46. *Sā. Bhā.* 1. 1. 5 (FW 48, 7-10) :

anupalabdhe ca devatādāv arthe 'narthakaṃ saṃjñākaraṇam aśakyaṃ ca. viśeṣan pratipattuṃ hi saṃjñāḥ kriyante viśeṣāṃś coddiśya. tad viśeṣeṣv ajñāyamāneṣu ubhayam apy anavakḷptam. tasmād apauruṣeyaḥ śabdasya arthena saṃbandhaḥ.

50. *Śā. Bhā.* 1. 1. 5 (FW 30, 20-21) :

pratyakṣatodṛṣṭasaṃbandhaṃ yathā dhūmākṛtidarśanād agnyākṛtivijñānam.

52. *Śā. Bhā.* 1. 1. 5 (FW 38. 3-4) :

atha "gaur" ity atra kaḥ śabdaḥ ? gakāraukāravisarjanīyā iti bhagavān upavarṣaḥ.

53. *Śā. Bhā.* 1. 1. 5 (FW 40, 3-4) :

na gauṇo 'kṣareṣu nimittabhāvaḥ, tadbhāve bhāvāt tadabhāve cābhāvāt.

54. *Śā. Bhā.* 1. 1. 5 (FW 38, 13) :

pūrvavarṇajanitasaṃskārasahito 'ntyo varṇaḥ pratyāyaka ity adoṣaḥ.

55. *Śā Bhā.* 1. 1. 5 (FW 40, 1-2) :

akṣarebhyaḥ saṃskāraḥ, samskārād arthapratipattir iti bhavanty arthapratipattāv akṣarāṇi nimittam.

56. *Śā. Bhā.* 1. 1. 5 (FW 40, 7-10) :

na ca pratyakṣo gakārādibhyo 'nyo gośabda iti, bhedadarśanābhāvād abhedadarśanāc ca. gakārādīni hi pratyakṣāṇi. tasmād "gaur" iti gakārādivisarjanīyāntaṃ padam akṣarāṇy eva. na tebhyo vyatiriktam anyat padaṃ nāma iti.—

81. *Śā. Bhā.* 1. 1. 5 (FW 30, 8) :

avyapadeśyaṃ ca naḥ pratyakṣam.

CHAPTER IV

13. *Śā. Bhā.* 1. 1. 5 (FW 34, 17-22) :

pauruṣeye hi sati saṃbandhe yaḥ pratyayaḥ, tasya mithyābhāva āśaṅkyeta. parapratyayo hi tadā syāt. atha śabde bruvati kathaṃ mithyā iti ? na hi tadānīm anyataḥ puruṣād avagamaḥ. "bravīti" ity ucyate "avabodhayati, budhyamānasya nimittam bhavati" iti. śabda cen nimittabhūte svayam avabudhyate, kathaṃ vipralabdhaṃ brūyān "naitad evam" iti.

14. *Śā. Bhā.* 1. 1. 5 (FW 24, 8-12) :

yac ca nāma jñānam utpannaṃ na viparyeti, na tac chakyate vaktuṃ "naitad evam" iti. "yathā vijñāyate na tathā bhavati; yathaitan na vijñāyate, tathaitad" iti. anyad asya hṛdaye, anyad vāci syāt. evaṃ vadato viruddham idam avagamyate "asti nāsti ca" iti.

15. *Śā. Bhā* 1.1.5 (FW 26, 4-5. 18-21) :

yad anyaviṣayaṃ jñānam anyasaṃprayoge bhavati. na tat pratyakṣam. . . . prayatnena anvicchanto na ced doṣam upalabhemahi, pramānābhāvād aduṣṭam iti manyemahi. tasmād yasya ca duṣṭaṃ karaṇaṃ yatra ca mithyeti pratyayaḥ, sa eva asamīcīnaḥ pratyayo nānya iti.

17. *Sā. Bhā.* 1.1.5 (FW 24, 7-8) :

avyatirekaś ca bhavati tasya jñānasya.

18. *Śā. Bhā.* 1.1.5 (FW 24, 12-14) :

tasmāt tat pramāṇam, anapekṣatvāt. na hy evaṃ sati pratyayāntaram apekṣitavyaṃ puruṣāntaraṃ vā. svayaṃpratyayo hy asau.

19. *Śā. Bhā* 1.1.5 (FW 32, 9) :

abhāvo 'pi pramāṇābhāvo "nāsti" ity asyārthasyāsaṃnikṛṣṭasya.

Śā. Bhā. 1.1.5 (FW 42, 18-19):

pratyakṣasya pramāṇasya abhāvāt tatpūrvakatvāc cetareṣām.

20. *Śā. Bhā.* 1.1.5 (FW 48, 17-20) :

na syāt pramāṇam, yadi pañcaiva pramāṇāny abhaviṣyan. yena yena hi pramīyate, tat tat pramāṇam, śabdenāpi pramīyate, tataḥ śabdo 'pi pramāṇam, yathaiva pratyaksam.

21. *Śā Bhā.* 1.1.2 (FW 16, 15-20. 23):

nanv atathābhūtam apy artham brūyāc codanā, yathā yatkiṃcana laukikaṃ vacanaṃ "nadyās tīre phalāni santi" iti. tat tathyam api bhavati, vitatham api bhavatīti.

ucyate : vipratiṣiddham - idam abhidhīyate "bravīti ca vitathaṃ ca" iti. bravīti ity ucyate 'vabodhayati, budhyamānasya nimittaṃ bhavati iti. yasmiṃś ca nimittabhūte saty avabudhyate, so 'vabodhayati.

22. *Śā. Bhā.* 1.1. 5 (FW 54, 14-15):

na cādṛṣṭapūrve smṛtir bhavati.

24. *Śā. Bhā.* 1.1.2 (FW 16, 12-14):

codanā hi bhūtaṃ bhavantaṃ bhaviṣyantaṃ sūkṣmaṃ vyavahitaṃ viprakṛṣtam ity evaṃjātīyakam arthaṃ śaknoty avagamayitum, nānyat, kiṃcanendriyam.

25. *Sā. Bhā.* 1.1.2 (FW 16,9) ;

codanā iti kriyāyāḥ pravartakaṃ vacanam āhuḥ.

37. *Śā. Bhā.* 1.1.2 (FW 18, 20-20, 2):

api ca puruṣavacanasādharmyād vedavacanaṃ vitatham iti anumānam. pratyakṣas tu vedavacane pratyayaḥ. na cānumānaṃ pratyakṣavirodhi pramāṇaṃ bhavati.

38. *Śa. Bhā.* 1.1.2. (FW 18, 11-15):

upadeśo hi vyāmohād api bhavati. asati vyāmohe vedād api bhavati. api ca pauruṣeyād vacanād "evam ayaṃ puruṣo veda" iti bhavati pratyayo, na "evam ayam artha" iti. viplavate khalv api kaścit puruṣakṛtād vacanāt pratyayaḥ. na tu vedavacanasya mithyātve kiṃcana pramāṇaṃ asti.

41. *Śa. Bhā.* 1.1.2 (FW 18, 3-5):

yat tu laukikaṃ vacanaṃ, tac cet pratyayitāt puruṣād indriyaviṣayaṃ vā, avitatham eva tat. athāpratyayitāt puruṣād anindriyaviṣayam vā, tat puruṣabuddhiprabhavam apramāṇam.

CHAPTER V

2. *Mī. sū* 1.1.1 (FW 10, 2):

athāto dharmajijñāsā

3. *Śā. Bhā.* 1.1.1 (FW 14, 21-16, 2):

dharmaḥ prasiddho vā syād aprasiddho vā. sa cet prasiddho, na jijñāsyaḥ. athāprasiddho, natarām. tad etad anarthakaṃ dharmajijñāsāprakaraṇam.

5. *Śā. Bhā.* 1.1.1 (FW 16, 3-6):

athavā arthavat. dharmaṃ prati hi vipratipannā bahuvidaḥ. kecid anyaṃ dharmam āhuḥ, kecid anyam. sò 'yam avicārya pravartamānaḥ kaṃcid eva upādadāno vihanyeta anarthaṃ 'ca ṛcchet. tasmād dharmo jijñāsitavyaḥ. sa hi niḥśreyasena puruṣaṃ saṃyunakti iti pratijānīmahe.

17 *Śa Bhā.* 1.1.1. (FW 12,11-14):

atikramiṣyāma imam āmnāyam. anatikrāmanto vedam arthavantaṃ santam anarthakaṃ kalpayema. dṛṣṭo hi tasyārthaḥ karmāvabodhanaṃ nāma. na ca tasya adhyayanamātrāt tatrabhavanto yājñikāḥ phalaṃ samāmananti.

18. *Śā Bhā.* 1.1.1 (FW 12, 8):

vedam adhītya snāyāt

19. *Mī. sū.* 1.1.1 (FW 10, 2):

athāto dharmajijñāsā

25. *Śā. Bhā.* 1.1.5 (FW 40,4-7):

athāpi gauṇaḥ syāt, na "gauṇaḥ śabdo mā bhūd"ity etāvatā pratyakṣādibhir anavagamyamāno 'rthaḥ śakyaḥ parikalpayitum. na hy "agnir māṇavaka" ity ukte 'gniśabdo gauṇo mā bhūd iti "jvalana eva māṇavaka" ity adhyavasīyate.

(Ass I-VII; Ānandāśrama Sanskrit Series 97, Vol. I-VII. The first Arabic figure refers to the page and the following to the lines.)

CHAPTER II

5. *Śā. Bhā.* 6.8.27 (ASS V, 366, 12-14) :

लोके कर्मार्थलक्षणं भवति, न शब्दलक्षणम् । यथाऽर्थस्तथा क्रियते, न यथा शब्दः । वेदे तु शब्देनैवार्थोऽवगम्यते, तथैवानुष्ठेयमिति । तस्माद्विद्यमानेऽपि कर्तव्यम् ।

7. *Śā. Bhā.* 6.1.2 (ASS V, 180, 9) :

प्रीत्यर्थं हि पुरुषो यतते ।

8. *Śā. Bhā.* 9.1.9 (ASS VI, 75, 14);

द्रव्यदेवतं हि भूतं, भावयितव्यो यजत्यर्थः ।

15. *Śā. Bhā.* 2.1.3 (ASS II, 355, 10-13) :

येषां शब्दानामुच्चारणोत्पत्तौ स्वेऽर्थे प्रयुज्यमानानां रूपमुपलभ्यते, यत् सकृदुत्पन्नं कालान्तरं तिष्ठति, न क्रियेवोत्पन्नमात्रं विनश्यतीत्यर्थः । तानि नामानि । ते द्रव्यगुणशब्दाः । ईदृशो द्रव्यगुणशब्दानामर्थः ।

27. *Śā. Bhā.* 2.2.25 (ASS III, 109, 3-7.8-9) :

अपि च कृषेर्नादृष्टमिति तत्सादृश्याद्धोमादपि नादृष्टं भवेत् । कृषिसादृश्याद्वा व्रीहिरेव भवेत्, नेर्ं द्रयम् । तस्मान्नैवंजातीयकेष्वेतद्भवति दृष्टाददृष्टसिद्धिरिति । कथं तर्हि होमान्न्याय्यं फलमिति । उच्यते । शब्देनावगम्यते तत्फलं, यतः फलमिति शब्द आह ततो न्याय्यम्...... तस्माद्धोमात्फलमिति न्याय्यम् । दध्नः फलमिति चान्याय्यम् ।

29. *Śā. Bhā.* 2.2.26 (ASS III, 114, 5-115, 1; 115, 2; 117, 1; 117, 3) :

होममाश्रितो गुणः फलं साधयिष्यति । यथा राजपुरुषो राजानमाश्रितो राजकर्म करोतीति । तस्माद्दध्नः फलं, य इन्द्रियकामः स दध्ना कुर्यादि-

न्द्रियमिति ।...फलसाधनस्य दध्न इतिकर्तव्यताकाङ्क्षत्वात् ।...तस्मा-
दध्नः फलमिति ।...तेन दध्नो होमेन संबध्यमानात् फलं भविष्यतीति ।

30. *Śā. Bhā.* 2.2.26 (ASS III, 111, 2-3) :
अग्निहोत्रं जुहुयात्स्वर्गकाम इत्यत्र कर्मसमभिव्याहृतं फलं स्वर्गकामो होमेन कुर्यादिति ।

33. *Śā. Bhā.* 6.1.1. (ASS V, 176, 2-5; 177, 9-11) :
कौशेयानि सूक्ष्माणि वासांसि स्वर्गः, चन्दनानि स्वर्गः, द्व्यष्टवर्षाः स्त्रियः स्वर्ग इति । यद्यत्प्रीतिमद्द्रव्यं तत्तत्स्वर्गशब्देनोच्यते । तेन सामानाधिकरण्यात्प्रीतिमद्द्रव्यं स्वर्ग इति मन्यामहे ।...
ननु स्वर्गशब्दो लोके प्रसिद्धो विशिष्टे देशे । यस्मिन्नोष्णं, न शीतं, न क्षुद्, न तृष्णा, नारतिः, न ग्लानिः, पुण्यकृत एव प्रेत्य तत्र गच्छन्ति नान्ये ।

34. *Śā. Bhā.* 6.1.1 (ASS V, 177, 14-16; 177, 22-178, 1)
न तत्र प्रमाणमस्ति, सिद्धा एवंजातीयकाः सन्ति, ते च दृष्ट्वाऽऽचक्षीरन्निति । तस्मादेवंजातीयको देश एव नास्ति ।...
तेन देशेन व्यवहाराभावात्कुतस्तस्याभिधायकः स्वर्गशब्दो भविष्यति ।

35. *Śā. Bhā.* 6.1.2 (ASS V, 181, 11-13) ;
तस्मादनर्थको मा भूदिति स्वर्गस्य कर्तव्यता गम्यते । पुरुषप्रयत्नश्च यागविशिष्ट इति यागस्तस्य करणं स्यात् । तस्मात्सुष्ठूक्तं यागो गुणभूतः, स्वर्गः प्रधानभूत इति ।

Śā. Bhā. 6.1.3 (ASS V, 183, 27-184, 2) :
इष्टमर्थं प्रत्यनुष्ठानं भवति । स्वर्गकामस्य च स्वर्ग इष्टः । तदनुष्ठानविशेषग्रहणार्थमेव स्वर्गकामविशेषणग्रहणमिति निरवद्यम् ।

36. *Śā. Bhā.* 6.1.2 (ASS V, 180, 7-9) :
इह पुनः स्वर्गशब्दः एव प्रीतेरभिधाता । प्रीतिवचनश्चेत्, यागो गुणभूतः प्रीतिः प्रधानम् । कुतः । तादर्थ्यात्पुरुषप्रयत्नस्य । प्रीत्यर्थं हि पुरुषो यतते ।

37. *Śā. Bhā.* 4.3.15 (ASS V, 72, 6-8) :
प्रीतिर्हि स्वर्गः । सर्वश्च प्रीतिं प्रार्थयते । किमतो यद्यवम् । अविशेषवचनः शब्दो न विशेषे व्यवस्थापितो भविष्यति ।

38. *Śā. Bhā.* 4.3.16 (ASS V, 72,11) :
भवति चानादिष्टफले कर्मणि स्वर्गः फलमिति ।

39. *Śā. Bhā.* 4.3.15 (ASS V, 72, 5-6) :
स स्वर्गः स्यात्सर्वान्प्रत्यविशिष्टत्वात् । सर्वे हि पुरुषाः स्वर्गकामा : ।

40. *Śā. Bhā.* 10.4.23 (ASS VI, 380, 7) :
सूक्तभाजो हविर्भाजश्च देवताः ।

41. *Śā. Bhā.* 9.1.9 (ASS VI, 79, 13-15) :

तस्मान्न किंचिदन्यार्थदर्शनं पुरुषविधतां देवतायामिदं ख्यापयतीति । न चेदं भोजनम् । न हि देवता भुङ्क्ते । तस्माद्भोजनस्य तदर्थत्वादिति तदसद्वचनम् ।

Śā. Bhā. 3.2.37 (ASS IV, 187, 5-6) :
न हि माद्यन्ति देवताः ।

Śā. Bhā. 9.1.9 (ASS VI, 79, 23-24) :
यदुक्तं, स्मृत्युपचारान्यार्थदर्शनैरीशाना देवतेत्यवगम्यत इति । तन्न ।

Śā. Bhā. 9.1.9 (ASS VI, 80, 3-5) :
यदुक्तम्, अन्यार्थदर्शनमीशानां देवतां ख्यापयति, इन्द्रो दिव इन्द्र ईशे इत्येवमादीति । तत्प्रत्यक्षामनीशानां देवतामुपलभ्याध्यवस्यामो भाक्त एष शब्द इति ।

42. *Śā. Bhā.* 6.1.5 (ASS V, 186,1-2; 5-6) :

न चैतदस्ति, तिर्यगादीनामप्यधिकार इति । कस्य तर्हि ...न देवानाम् । देवतान्तराभावात् । न ह्यात्मानमुद्दिश्य त्यागः संभवति । त्याग एवासौ न स्यात् ।

43. *Śā. Bhā.* 6.1.2 (ASS V, 180, 11) :
यस्माद्द्रव्यदेवताक्रिये यजतिशब्दो वर्तते ।

44. *Śā. Bhā.* 8.1.32 (ASS VI, 19, 4-5) :

विप्रतिपत्तौ हविषा नियम्येत । विप्रतिपत्तावेतस्यां हविर्देवतयोः, हविषा विध्यन्तो नियम्येत ।

45. *Śā. Bhā.* 9.1.9 (ASS VI, 75, 14; 76, 1-3) :

गुणत्वे देवताश्रुतिः । द्रव्यदेवतं हि भूतं,...
तत्र यद्यपि देवतार्थता यागस्य गम्यते, फलार्थताऽपि तेन न प्रतिषिध्यते । फलं च पुरुषार्थः। पुरुषार्था च नः प्रवृत्तिः । न चासौ देवतायाः ।

46. *Śā. Bhā.* 6.3.18 (ASS V, 255, 14-16) :

न देवताग्निशब्दाक्रियाणामपचारे प्रतिनिधिना भवितव्यमिति । कुतः । अन्यार्थसंयोगात् । प्रतिनिधीयमानमन्यदेतेभ्यः । अन्यच्च तेषामर्थं न शक्नुयात्कर्तुम् ।

Śā. Bhā. 10.4.23 (ASS VI, 379, 8-11) :

विधिशब्देनैव—अग्निशब्देनोद्दिष्टव्या, नान्येन शुच्यादिनेति । कुतः । तेन चोदना । तेन—विधिशब्देनास्य हविषः संबन्धचोदना भवति । कथमिव। आग्नेयः कर्तव्य इत्यग्निरस्य देवता कर्तव्येत्यर्थ ।

49. *Śā. Bhā.* 10.4.23 (ASS VI, 379, 14-380, 2) :

स्मर्यते च कालवाचिनां देवतात्वं, कालेभ्यो भवति, मासो देवता, संवत्सरो देवता, इति ।

50. *Śā. Bhā.* 10.4.23 (ASS VI, 379, 12-13) :

एकं तावन्मतं, या एता इतिहासपुराणेष्वग्न्याद्याः संकीर्त्यन्ते नाकसदः, ता देवता इति ।

51. *Śā. Bhā.* 10.4.23 (ASS VI, 380, 5-8) :

किंच सामान्यवचनस्य शब्दस्य लौकिके व्यवहारेऽभावादर्थस्याप्रसिद्धिः स्यात् । तस्मात्सूक्तभाजो हविर्भाजश्च देवताः ।

52. *Śā. Bhā.* 10.4.23 (ASS VI, 380, 25-381, 3.5-8.12-13) :

देवतायाश्च यज्ञसाधनभावो न रूपेण भवति । केन तर्हि । संबन्धिना शब्देन । यथा, अध्वर्युर्हस्ताभ्यामुपकरोति, एवं देवता शब्देनोपकरोति । यथा, होतुः पाणौ द्विर्लेपेनोपस्तृणातीति पाणिसंबन्धेऽपि होतैवोपकरोति, एवं संबन्धिना शब्देनोपकुर्वती देवतोपकारिणी गम्यते । देवतायामप्युपकारिण्यां चोदितायां शब्दस्यैव यज्ञे समवायः ।...
किं तर्हि । शब्द एव हविषा सबध्यते । तत्संबन्धादर्थोऽपिदेवता भविष्यति । यस्य हि शब्दो हविषा तादर्थ्येन संबध्यते, सा देवता ।

शब्दे कार्यस्यासंभवादर्थे कार्यं विज्ञायते। इह तु शब्द एव कार्यं सम्भवति। तस्मान्नार्थप्रत्यायनार्थः शब्द इति।...
नन्वेवं शब्द एव देवता प्राप्नोति। अत्रोच्यते। नैतदस्माभिः परिहर्तव्यम्। न हीदमुच्यमानमस्मत्पक्षं बाधते।

55. *Śā. Bhā.* 9.1.9 (ASS VI, 76, 15-17) :
य आलोचनमात्रेण मन्त्रार्थवादान् पश्यन्ति, तेषां तत्स्मृतिमूलम्। ये पुनर्निपुणतः पश्यन्ति, तेषां तद्बाधितमपि च कस्यचित्स्मृतिमूलं भवति। तस्मात्तत एव स्मृतिः।

57. *Śā. Bhā.* 2.1.5 (ASS II, 377, 1-2) :
यत्र समवेतमासीत्, तद्विनष्टं द्रव्यम्। तस्य विनाशात्तदपि विनष्टमित्यवगम्यते। आश्रयोऽप्यविनष्ट इति चेन्न। भस्मोपलम्भनात्।

58. *Śā. Bhā.* 2.1.5 (ASS II, 372, 2-3) :
यदाश्रयं देशान्तरं प्रापयति, तत्कर्मेत्युच्यते।

63. *Śā. Bhā.* 2.1.1 (ASS II, 340, 8-341, 1.5) :
अतो यस्तस्य वाचकः शब्दस्ततोऽपूर्वं प्रतीयत इति। तेन भावशब्दा अपूर्वस्य चोदका इति ब्रूमः। न तु कश्चिच्छब्दः साक्षादपूर्वस्य वाचकोऽस्ति।...तस्माद् भावार्थाः कर्मशब्दा अपूर्वं चोदयन्तीति।

64. *Śā. Bhā.* 2.1.4 (ASS II, 357, 1-3; 358, 9-10) :
येषां तु शब्दानामुच्चारणोत्पत्तौ स्वेऽर्थे प्रयोगो न विद्यते। प्रयोगकाले येषामर्थो नोपलभ्यत इत्यर्थः। तान्याख्यातानीति भावशब्दान् पर्यायशब्देनोपदिशति। कथं पर्यायशब्दता भावशब्दानाम्।...एष विनिगमनायां हेतुर्येन भावशब्दा एवापूर्वस्य चोदकाः, न द्रव्यगुणशब्दा इति।

65. *Śā. Bhā.* 2.1.1 (ASS II, 340, 7-8) :
यस्य च शब्दस्यार्थेन फलं साध्यते, तेनापूर्वं कृत्वा नान्यथेति ततोऽपूर्वं गम्यते।

67. *Śā. Bhā.* 2.1.4 (ASS II, 357, 10-13) :
किंच आश्रितत्वात् प्रयोगस्य। एतेषां प्रयोगः पुरुषेणाऽऽश्रितो भवति, पुरुषसंबद्धा भावनोच्यते। पुरुषं हि वदति। भावयेदिति। तेन स्वर्गकामो यजेतेति पुरुषोऽपि प्रतीयते, यागोऽपि संबन्धोऽपि।

69. *Śā. Bhā.* 2.1.5 (ASS II, 378, 2-3):
तस्माद्गुणी यजिः, तस्य भङ्गित्वादपूर्वमस्तीति ।

70. *Śā. Bhā.* 2.2.1 (ASS III, 8, 6-7. 9-11):
तस्माद्भिन्नानि वाक्यानि, प्रतिशब्दमपूर्वभेद इति ।...प्रयोजनं—पूर्वपक्षे समुदायादपूर्वं, सिद्धान्ते तु यागस्य फलवत्त्वादितरयोर्गुणभावः ।

71. *Śā. Bhā.* 2.1.5 (ASS II, 358, 16-359, 1) :
चोदनेत्यपूर्वं ब्रूमः । अपूर्वं पुनरस्ति, यत आरम्भः शिष्यते स्वर्गकामो यजेतेति । इतरथा हि विधानमनर्थकं स्यात् ।

CHAPTER III

4. *Śā. Bhā.* 1.1.22 (ASS I, 109, 1-2) :
ननु वायुकारणकः स्यादिति वायुरुद्गतः संयोगविभागैः शब्दो भवतीति ।

5. *Śā. Bhā.* 1.1.14 (ASS I, 96, 2-3) :
यदपरं कारणमुक्तं शब्दं कुरु मा कार्षीरिति व्यवहर्तारः प्रयुञ्जते ।

6. *Mī. Sū.* 1.1.16 (ASS I, 99, 4) :
वर्णान्तरमविकारः ।

Śā Bhā. 1.1.16 (ASS I, 100, 1-2) :
शब्दान्तरमिकाराद्यकारः ।

7. *Śā. Bhā.* 1.1.20 (ASS I, 105,5) :
अष्टकृत्वो गोशब्द उच्चरित इति ।

9. *Śā. Bhā.* 1.1. 17 (ASS I, 101,1-8) :

यच्चैतद्बहुभिर्भेरीमाधमद्भिः शब्दमुच्चारयद्भिर्महाञ्शब्द उपलभ्यते, तेन प्रतिपुरुषं शब्दावयवप्रचय इति गम्यते । नैवम् । निरवयवो हि शब्दः अवयवभेदानवगमान्निरवयवत्वाच्च महत्त्वानुपपत्तिः । अतो न वर्धते शब्दः मृदुरेकेन बहुभिश्चोच्चार्यमाणे तान्येवाक्षराणि कर्णशष्कुलीमण्डलस्य सर्वां नेमिं व्याप्नुवद्भिः संयोगविभागैर्नैरन्तर्येणानेकशो ग्रहणान्महानिवावयववानिवोपलभ्यन्ते । संयोगविभागा नैरन्तर्येण क्रियमाणाः शब्दमभिव्यञ्जन्तो नादशब्दवाच्याः तेन नादस्यैषा वृद्धिर्न शब्दस्येति ।

10. *Śā. Bhā.* 1.1.20 (ASS I, 106, 6-7) :

ह्यस्तनस्य शब्दस्य विनाशादन्योऽद्यतन इति चेत् । नैष विनष्टः ।

34. *SV Ākṛtivādaḥ* 3-4 :

जातिमेवाकृतिं प्राहुर्व्यक्तिराक्रियते यया ।
सामान्यं तच्च पिण्डानामेकबुद्धिनिबन्धनम् ॥३॥
तन्निमित्तं च यत्किञ्चित् सामान्यं शब्दगोचरम् ।
सर्व एवेच्छतीत्येवमविरोधोऽत्र वादिनाम् ॥४॥

35. *Śā. Bhā.* 1.1.19 (ASS I, 104, 2-105, 3) :

गोशब्द उच्चरिते सर्वगवीषु युगपत्प्रत्ययो भवति । अत आकृतिवचनोऽयम् । न चाऽऽकृत्या शब्दस्य संबन्धः शक्यते कर्तुम् । निर्दिश्य ह्याकृतिं कर्ता संबध्नीयात् । गोपिण्डे च बहूनामाकृतीनां सद्भावाच्छब्दमन्तरेण गोशब्दवाच्यां विभक्तामाकृतिं केन प्रकारेणोपदेक्ष्यति । नित्ये तु सति गोशब्दे बहुकृत्व उच्चरितः श्रुतपूर्वश्चान्यासु गोव्यक्तिष्वन्वयव्यतिरेकाभ्यामाकृतिवचनमवगमयिष्यति तस्मादपि नित्यः ॥

39. *Śā. Bhā.* 1.3.33 (ASS II, 247, 17-248, 1) :

यदि च विशिष्टा, पूर्वतरं विशेषणमवगम्येत । न ह्यप्रतीते विशेषणे विशिष्टं केचन प्रत्येतुमर्हन्तीति ।

40. *Śā. Bhā.* 1.3.33 (ASS II, 264, 2-3) :

तस्माच्छब्द आकृतिप्रत्ययस्य निमित्तम् । आकृतिप्रत्ययो व्यक्तिप्रत्ययस्येति ।

41. *Śā. Bhā.* 1.3.33 (ASS II, 248, 5-264, 1) :

यदि चात्राऽऽकृतिः प्रतीयते शब्देन, तदा व्यक्तिरपि पदार्थ इति न शक्यते वदितुम् । कुतः । आकृतिर्हि व्यक्त्या नित्यसंबद्धा, संबन्धिन्यां च तस्यामवगतायां संबन्ध्यन्तरमवगम्यते । तदेतदात्मप्रत्यक्षं, यच्छब्द उच्चरिते व्यक्तिः प्रतीयत इति । किं शब्दादुताऽऽकृतेरिति विभागो न प्रत्यक्षः सोऽन्वयव्यतिरेकाभ्यामवगम्यते । अन्तरेणापि शब्दं य आकृतिमवबुध्येत, अवबुध्येतैवासौ व्यक्तिम् । यस्तूच्चरितेऽपि शब्दे मानसादपचारात् कदाचिदाकृतिं नोपलभेत न जातुचिदसाविमां व्यक्तिमवगच्छेत ।

42. *Śā. Bhā.* 1.3.33 (ASS II, 265, 4-5) :

तस्मात् साध्वेतद्यत् प्रतीते विशेषणे विशिष्टः प्रतीयत इति ।

43. *Śā. Bhā.* 1.3.33 (ASS II, 247, 7-9) :
तस्मात्तत्र न वर्तिष्यते यदि यत्र प्रयोगो दृष्टस्तत्र वृत्तिः, अद्य जातायां गवि प्रथमप्रयोगो न प्राप्नोति तत्रादृष्टत्वात् ।

44. *Śā. Bhā.* 1.3.33 (ASS II, 247, 11-12) :
तस्मान्न प्रयोगापेक्षो गोशब्दो व्यक्तिवचन इति शक्यत आश्रयितुम् ।

45. *Śā. Bhā.* 1.3.16 (ASS II, 173, 3; 175, 7-8) :
विधीयतेऽनेनेति विधानं शब्दः ।...न तस्याऽऽकृतिवचनता न्याय्या न व्यक्तिवचनतेति ।

58. *Mī. Sū.* 1.1.16 (ASS I, 99, 4) :
वर्णान्तरमविकारः ।

59. *Śā. Bhā.* 1.1.16 (ASS I, 100, 1-2) :
शब्दान्तरमिकाराद्यकारः ।

60. *Śā. Bhā.* 1.1.18 (ASS I, 102, 6-8) :
तदुक्तं सदृश इति चावगते व्यामोहात्प्रत्ययो व्यावर्तेत शालाशब्दान्मालाप्रत्यय इव ।

61. *Śā. Bhā.* 1.3.24 (ASS II, 182, 6) :
गौर्गावी गोणी गोपोतलिका इत्येवमादयः शब्दा उदाहरणम् । गोशब्दो यथा सास्नादिमति प्रमाणं, किं तथा गाव्यादयोऽप्युत नेति संदेहः ।

Śā. Bhā. 1.3.26 (ASS II, 214, 2-3) :
तस्मादमीषामेकोऽनादिरन्येऽपभ्रंशाः ।

Śā. Bhā. 1.3.26 (ASS II, 214, 1-2) :
सादृश्यात्सा धुशब्देऽप्यवगते प्रत्ययोऽवकल्प्यते ।

62. *Śā. Bhā.* 1.3.29 (ASS II, 228, 11-12) :
एवं गाव्यादिदर्शनाद्गोशब्दस्मरणं ततः सास्नादिमानवगम्यते ।

63. *Śā. Bhā.* 1.3.24 (ASS II, 182,8-183,1.4) :
किमत्रैकः शब्दोऽविच्छिन्नपारम्पर्योऽर्थाभिधायी, इतरेऽपभ्रंशाः, उत सर्वेऽनादयः । सर्वं इति ब्रूमः ।...तस्मात्सर्वे साधवः ।

Śā. Bhā. 1.3.25 (ASS II, 212, 2-213, 1) :

ततोऽपराधात्प्रवृत्ता गाव्यादयो भवेयुर्न नियोगतोऽविच्छिन्नपारम्पर्या एवेति ।

64. *Śā. Bhā.* 1.3.28 (ASS II, 228, 2-3) :

तदशक्तिरेषां गम्यते। गोशब्दमुच्चारयितुकामेन केनचिदशक्त्या गावीत्यु-च्चारितम् ।

65. *Śā. Bhā.* 1.3.26 (ASS II, 214, 2-3) :

तस्मादमीषामेकोऽनादिरन्येऽपभ्रंशाः ।

66. *Śā. Bhā.* 1.3.26 (ASS II, 214, 3-4) :

हस्तः करः पाणिरित्येवमादिषु त्वभियुक्तोपदेशादनादिरमीषामर्थेन संबन्ध इति ।

68. *Śā. Bhā.* 1.1.17 (ASS I, 101, 2-3) :

निरवयवो हि शब्दः अवयवभेदानवगमान्निरवयवत्वाच्च महत्त्वानुपपत्तिः ।

69. *Śā. Bhā.* 1.1.15 (ASS I, 99, 1-2) :

अपि चैकरूप्ये सति देशभेदेन कामं देशा एव भिन्ना न तु शब्दः ।

70. *SV Ākṛtivādaḥ* 5-7 :

अनादिव्यवहारत्वमादिमद् वस्तुसंश्रयम् ।
प्रत्याख्येयम्, घटत्वादिजातौ व्यक्तिभ्रमो हि सः ॥५॥

स्थिते कूटस्थनित्यत्वे व्यवहारस्य नित्यता ।
कूटस्थेन विनैतेन न तस्यालम्बनं भवेत् ॥६॥

प्रसिद्धत्वाद् ऋते सर्वो व्यवहारो हि नेष्यते ।
तस्माद् वेदप्रमाणार्थं नित्यत्वमिह साध्यते ॥७॥

SV Śabdanityatādhikaraṇa 290-305 :

यत्नतः प्रतिषेध्या नः पुरुषाणां स्वतन्त्रता ।
वर्णानामपि नन्वेवमकौटस्थ्येऽपि सेत्स्यति ॥२९०॥

नित्येषु सत्सु वर्णेषु व्यवहारात् क्रमोदयः ।
घटादिरचना यद्वन्नित्येषु परमाणुषु ॥२९१॥
तदभावे हि निर्मूला रचना नावधार्यते ।

अणकल्पाश्च वर्णांशा न सन्तीत्युपपादितम् ॥२९२॥

परैरुक्तान् ब्रवीमीति विवक्षा चेदृशी ध्रुवम् ।
तथा च नित्यतापत्तिः, न चान्यच्चिह्नमस्ति वः ॥२९३॥

तज्जातीयत्वसादृश्ये निषिद्धे, यत्तु सम्भवेत् ।
शब्दत्वेन सजातित्वं तुल्यं शब्दान्तरेषु तत् ॥२९४॥

जात्या यथा घटादीनां व्यवहारोपलक्षणम् ।
तथैव चानुपूर्व्यादेर्जातिद्वारेण सेत्स्यति ॥२९५॥

ताल्वादिजातयस्तावत् सर्वपुंसां व्यवस्थिताः ।
वक्ता तावद् ध्वनींस्ताभिरुपलक्ष्य निरस्यति ॥२९६॥

तेषां च जातयो भिन्नाः शब्दाभिव्यक्तिहेतवः ।
यावद्वर्णं प्रवर्तन्ते व्यक्तयो वा तदन्विताः ॥२९७॥

तत्र ताल्वादिसंयोगविभागक्रमपूर्वकम् ।
ध्वनीनामानुपूर्व्यं स्याज्जात्यः चोभयनित्यता ॥२९८॥

यथैव भ्रमणादीनां भागैर्जात्या च लक्षितैः ।
क्रमानुवृत्तिरेवं स्यात् ताल्वादिध्वनिवर्णभाक् ॥२९९॥

व्यक्तीनामेव वा सौक्ष्म्याज्जातिधर्मावधारणम् ।
तद्वशेन च वर्णानां व्यापित्वेऽपि क्रमग्रहः ॥३००॥

एवं ध्वनिगुणान् सर्वान्नित्यत्वेन व्यवस्थितान् ।
वर्णा अनुपतन्तः स्युरर्थभेदावबोधिनः ॥३०१॥

आनुपूर्वी च वर्णानां ह्रस्वदीर्घप्लुताश्च ये ।
कालस्य प्रविभागास्तैर्जायन्ते ध्वन्युपाधयः ॥३०२॥

कालश्चैको विभुर्नित्यः, प्रविभक्तोऽपि गम्यते ।
वर्णवत्, सर्वभावेषु व्यज्यते केनचित् क्वचित् ॥३०३॥

वर्णेषु व्यज्यमानस्य तस्य प्रत्यायनाङ्गता ।
अन्यत्रापि तु सद्भावात् तत्स्वरूपस्य नित्यता ॥३०४॥

तस्मान्न पदधर्मोऽस्ति विनाशी कश्चिदीदृशः ।
तेन नित्यं पदं सिद्धं वर्णनित्यत्ववादिनाम् ॥३०५॥

73. *Śā Bhā*. 1.1.12 (ASS I, 91, 4-5) :
यदि विस्पष्टेन हेतुना शब्दस्य नित्यत्वं वक्तुं शक्ष्यामस्ततो नित्यप्रत्ययसामर्थ्यात्प्रयत्नेनाभिव्यज्यत इति भविष्यति ।

Śā. Bhā. 1.1.13 (ASS, 91, 9-10) :

अत्रापि यदि शक्ष्यामो नित्यतामस्य विस्पष्टं वक्तुं ।

77. *Śā. Bhā.* 1.1.20 (ASS I, 105, 5-106, 1.3-4) :

अष्टकृत्वो गोशब्द उच्चरित इति वदन्ति नाष्टौ गोशब्दा इति किमतो यद्येवम् । अनेन वचनेनावगम्यते प्रत्यभिजानन्तीति । वयं तावत्प्रत्यभिजानीमो न नः करणदौर्बल्यम् । एवमन्येऽपि प्रत्यभिजानन्ति । स एवाय-मिति । प्रत्यभिजानानाः प्रत्यभिजानन्ति चेद्वयमिवान्येऽपि नान्य इति वक्तुमर्हन्ति ।...

न चायमन्य इति प्रत्यक्षमन्यद्वा प्रमाणमस्ति ।

78. *Śā. Bhā.* 1.1.20 (ASS I, 106,5-6) :

न हि ते प्रत्यक्षे । अथ प्रत्यक्षे नित्ये एव ।

80. *Śā. Bhā.* 1.1.20 (ASS I, 106, 6-14) :

ह्यस्तनस्य शब्दस्य विनाशादन्योऽद्यतन इति चेत् । नैष विनष्टः । यत एनं पुनरुपलभामहे । न हि प्रत्यक्षदृष्टं मुहूर्तमदृष्ट्वा पुनरुपलभ्यमानं प्रत्यभिजानन्तो विनष्टं परिकल्पयन्ति । परिकल्पयन्तो द्वितीयसंदर्शने मातरि जायायां पितरि वा नाऽऽश्वस्युः । न ह्यनुपलम्भमात्रेण नास्तीत्यवगम्य नष्ट इत्येव कल्पयन्ति । अप्रमाणतायां विदितायां नास्तीत्यवगच्छामः । न हि प्रमाणे प्रत्यक्षे सत्यप्रमाणता स्यात् । अस्तीति पुनरव्यामोहेनावगम्यमाने न क्वचिदप्यभावः । न चासिद्धेऽभावे व्यामोहः । न च सिद्धोऽभावः । तस्मादसति व्यामोहे नाभावः ।

85. *Śā. Bhā.* 1.1.15 (ASS 99, 1-2) :

एकं च पुनराकाशम् । अतोऽपि न नानादेशेषु । अपि चैकरूप्ये सति देशभेदेन कामं देशा एव भिन्ना न तु शब्दः ।

87. *Śā. Bhā.* 1.1.16 (ASS I, 100, 2-3) :

न हि यकारं प्रयुञ्जाना इकारमुपाददते । यथा कटं चिकीर्षन्तो वीरणानि ।

Śā. Bhā. 1.1.22 (ASS I, 109, 4-8) :

नैतदेवम् । वायवीयश्चेच्छब्दो भवेद्वायोः संनिवेशविशेषः स्यात् । न च वायवीयानवयवाञ्शब्दे सतः प्रत्यभिजानीमो यथा पटस्य तन्तुमयान् ।

न चैवं भवति । स्याच्चेदेवं स्पर्शनेनोपलभेमहि । न च वायवीयानवयवाञ्शब्दगतान्स्पृशामः । तस्मान्न वायुकारणकः । अतो नित्यः ।

88. *Śā. Bhā.* 1.1.21 (ASS I, 108, 2-6) :

येषामनवगतोत्पत्तीनां द्रव्याणां भाव एव लक्ष्यते तेषामपि केषांचिदनित्यता गम्यते, येषां विनाशकारणमुपलभ्यते । यथाऽभिनवं पटं दृष्ट्वा । न चैनं क्रियमाणमुपलब्धवान् । अथवाऽनित्यत्वमवगच्छति रूपमेव दृष्ट्वा । तन्तुव्यतिषङ्गजनितोऽयं तन्तुव्यतिषङ्गविनाशात्तन्तुविनाशाद्वा विनश्यतीत्यवगच्छति । नैवं शब्दस्य किंचित्कारणमवगम्यते यद्विनाशाद्विनङ्क्ष्यतीत्यवगम्यते ।

95. *Śā. Bhā.* 1.1.18 (ASS I, 101, 10-102, 1) :

नित्यः शब्दो भवितुमर्हति । कुतः दर्शनस्य परार्थत्वात् । दर्शनमुच्चारणं तत्परार्थं परमर्थं प्रत्याययितुम् ।

CHAPTER IV

1. *Śā. Bhā.* 1.3.30 (ASS II, 231, 6-232, 3) :

य एव लौकिकाः शब्दास्त एव वैदिकाऽस्त एवैषामर्था इति । कुतः । प्रयोगचोदनाभावात् । एवं प्रयोगचोदना संभवति यदि त एव शब्दास्त एवार्थाः, इतरथा शब्दान्यत्वेऽर्थो न प्रतीयेत ।

2. *Śā. Bhā.* 1.3.30 (ASS II, 233,1-3) :

यदि चान्ये वैदिकास्तत उत्तानादीनामर्थो न गम्येत, तत्र नतरां शक्येताविज्ञातलक्षणं गोत्वं विज्ञातुम् ।

3. *Śā. Bhā.* 1.1.25 (ASS I, 116, 5-6) :

पदानि हि स्वं स्वं पदार्थमभिधाय निवृत्तव्यापाराणि । अथेदानीं पदार्था अवगताः सन्तो वाक्यार्थं गमयन्ति ।

4. *Śā. Bhā.* 1.1.25 (ASS I, 116, 10) :

विशिष्टार्थसंप्रत्ययश्च वाक्यार्थः ।

5. *Śā. Bhā.* 1.1.25 (ASS I, 117, 4-6) :

अपि चान्तरेणापि पदोच्चारणं यः शौक्ल्यमवगच्छत्यवगच्छत्येवासौ शुक्लगुणकम् । तस्मात्पदार्थप्रत्यय एव वाक्यार्थो नास्य पदसमुदायेन संबन्धः ।

6. *Śā. Bhā.* 1.1.25 (ASS I, 117, 10-11) :

एवं च सति गुणान्तरप्रतिषेधो न शब्दार्थ इत्येतदपि परिहृतं भवति ।

9. *Śā. Bhā.* 1.1.24 (ASS I, 110, 4-5; 111, 5-6);

यद्यप्यौत्पत्तिको नित्यः शब्दः संबन्धश्च तथाऽपि न चोदनालक्षणो धर्मः। चोदना हि वाक्यम् ।...

पदान्यमूनि प्रयुक्तानि तेषां नित्योऽर्थः । अप्रयुक्तश्च समुदायः । तस्मात्समुदायस्यार्थः कृत्रिमो व्यामोहो वा ।

10. *Śā. Bhā.* 1.1.25 (ASS I, 117, 1-3) :

भवति हि कदाचिदियमवस्था मानसादप्याघातात् । यदुच्चरितेभ्यः पदेभ्यो न पदार्था अवधार्यन्ते ।

11. *Mī. Sū.* 2.1.46 (ASS II, 431, 9-10) :

अर्थैकत्वादेकं वाक्यं साकाङ्क्षं चेद्विभागे स्यात् ।

12. *Śā. Bhā.* 1.1.18 (ASS I, 101, 10-102, 1) :

नित्यः शब्दो भवितुमर्हति । कुतः दर्शनस्य परार्थत्वात् । दर्शनमुच्चारणं तत्परार्थं परमर्थं प्रत्याययितुम् ।

16. *Śā. Bhā.* 1.1.25 (ASS I, 117, 1-2) :

भवति हि कदाचिदियमवस्था मानसादप्याघातात् ।

23. *Śā. Bhā.* 1.4.4 (ASS II, 285, 12-13) :

अविदितवेदनं च विधिरित्युच्यते ।

26. *Śā. Bhā.* 1.1.27 (ASS I, 120, 9) :

संनिकृष्टकालाः कृतका वेदा इदानींतनाः,

27. *Śā. Bhā.* 1.1.29 (ASS I, 122, 2) :

उक्तमस्माभिः शब्दपूर्वत्वमध्येतॄणाम् ।

28. *Śā. Bhā.* 1.1.30 (ASS I, 122, 5-6) :

नेयमर्थापत्तिः । अकर्तृभिरपि ह्येनामाचक्षीरन् ।

29. *Śā. Bhā.* 1.1.30 (ASS I, 123, 1-2. 3-5) :

प्रकर्षेण वचनमनन्यसाधारणं कठादिभिरनुष्ठितं स्यात्तथाऽपि हि समा-

ख्यातारो भवन्ति ।... स बहुशाखाध्यायिनां संनिधावेकशाखाध्याय्यन्या शाखामनधीयानस्तस्यां प्रकृष्टत्वादसाधारणमुपपद्यते विशेषणम् ।

30. *Śā. Bhā.* 1.1.31 (ASS I, 124, 5) :

परं तु श्रुतिसामान्यमात्रमिति ।

31. *Śā. Bhā.* 1.1.32 (ASS I, 125, 3-4) :

अपि च 'वनस्पतयः सत्रमासत' इत्येवमादयोऽपि नानुपपन्नाः स्तुतयो ह्येता सत्रस्य ।

Śā. Bhā. 1.1.32 (ASS, 124, 14-125, 1) :

कथमुन्मत्तबालवाक्यसदृशमिति वक्ष्यामः ।

32. *Śā. Bhā.* 1.1.32 (ASS I, 124, 10-11) :

विनियुक्तं हि दृश्यते परस्परेण संबन्धार्थम् ।

34. *Śā. Bhā.* 1.1.32 (ASS I, 125, 7-126, 1) ;

अपि चाविगीतः सुहृदुपदेशः सुप्रतिष्ठितः ।

35. *Śā. Bhā.* 1.3.1 (ASS II, 69, 11) ;

एवं तावत्कृत्स्नस्य वेदस्य प्रामाण्यमुक्तम् ।

36. *Śā. Bhā.* 2.1.33 (ASS II, 421, 5-6) :

मन्त्राश्च ब्राह्मणं च वेदः । तत्र मन्त्रलक्षण उक्ते परिशेषसिद्धत्वाद् ब्राह्मणलक्षणमवचनीयम् ।

40. *Śā. Bhā.* 1.3.4 (ASS II, 102, 6-104, 2) ;

लोभाद्वास आदित्समाना औदुम्बरीं कृत्स्नां वेष्टितवन्तः केचित् । तत्स्मृतेर्बीजम् । बुभुक्षमाणाः केचित्क्रीतराजकस्य भोजनमाचरितवन्तः । अपुंस्त्वं प्रच्छादयन्तश्चाष्टाचत्वारिंशद्वर्षाणि वेदब्रह्मचर्यं चरितवन्तः । तत एषा स्मृतिरित्यवगम्यते ।

'वैसर्जनहोमीयं वासोऽध्वर्युर्गृह्णाति' इति 'यूपहस्तिनो दानमाचरन्ति इति । तत्कर्तृसामान्यात् प्रमाणमिति प्राप्ते अप्रमाणं स्मृतिः । अत्रान्यन्मूलम् । लोभादाचरितवन्तः केचित्तत एषा स्मृतिः । उपपन्नतरं चैतत् ।

CHAPTER V

24. *Śā. Bhā.* 3.2.1 (ASS IV, 123, 7-10) :

यः शब्दादेवावगभ्यते, स प्रथमोऽर्थो मुख्यः। मुखमिव भवतीति मुख्य इत्युच्यते। यस्तु खलु प्रतीतादर्थात् केनचित्संबधेन गम्यते, स पश्चाद्भावाज्जघनमिव भवतीति जघन्यः। गुणसंबन्धाच्च गौण इति।

CHAPTER VI

1. *RV* 4.58.3 :

चत्वारि शृङ्गा त्रयो अस्य पादा द्वे शीर्षे सप्त हस्तासो अस्य।
त्रिधा बद्धो वृषभो रोरवीति महो देवो मर्त्यां आ विवेश॥

2. *Śā. Bhā* 1.2.46 (ASS II, 64, 7-11) :

चतस्रो होत्राः शृङ्गाणीवाऽस्य। त्रयोऽस्य पादा इति सवनाभिप्रायम्। द्वे शीर्षे इति पत्नी यजमानौ। सप्त हस्तास इति चछन्दांस्यभिप्रेत्य। त्रिधा बद्ध इति त्रिभिर्वेदैर्बद्धः। वृषभः कामान्वर्षतीति रोरवीति शब्दकर्मा, महो देवो मर्त्यानाविवेशेति मनुष्याधिकाराभिप्रायम्।

5. *Śā. Bhā.* 1.2.49 (ASS II, 66, 1-67, 1) :

विद्यमानोऽप्यर्थः प्रमादालस्यादिभिर्नोपलभ्यते। निगमनिरुक्तव्याकरणवशेन धातुतोऽर्थः कल्पयितव्यः।

7. *VP* 1.122 (130) :

अपि प्रयोक्तुरात्मानं शब्दमन्तरवस्थितम्।
प्राहुर्महान्तमृषभं येन सायुज्यमिष्यते॥

GLOSSARY OF SANSKRIT TERMS

Abhāva	Non-existence, absence, negation; *pramāṇa* indicating absence of another *pramāṇa*, i.e. *anupalabdhi*.
Adhyāya	Chapter.
Adhvaryu	One of the main officiating priests in the sacrifice.
Adṛṣṭa	Invisible; there is no concrete information about any invisible object available, but its presence is given in and through *śabda*.
Agni	Fire; brilliance; name of a deity.
Aikarūpya	Unity of form.
Ākāra	Form, 'structure', which is directly perceived.
Ākāśa	Ether.
Ākṛti	Specific form; 'proper object' permanently related to *śabda*. It is a determining factor of the individual, thus also of a class. Its function is ineffable in the *adṛṣṭa*.
Akṣara	Phoneme
Āmnāya	Tradition, traditional instruction.
Anādi	Without beginning (*anādinitya* beginninglessly eternal).
Anityatva	Impermanence.
Anubhūti	Direct experience which reveals the 'new', proper knowledge. Authentic hermeneutics is identical with *anubhūti* and not with reproduced knowledge as found in *smṛti*.
Anumāna	Inference, a *pramāṇa*.
Anupalabdhi	Non-perception, non-cognition; a *pramāṇa* which indicates non-existence through the absence of another *pramāṇa*.
Anupapanna	absurd
Apabhraṃśa	Corrupted.
Apauruṣeya	Not of human (or divine) origin.

Apūrva What previously did not exist, what is new; invisible power leading to an intended, though not foreseen consequence of a sacrificial act : *svarga.*

Artha Object; purpose; meaning.

Arthāpatti Presumption; a *pramāṇa.*

Arthavāda Explanatory proclamation of the object/purpose. It is not injunctive, but completes the *vidhi.*

Ātman Self; Invisible, lasting core of man's existence. It is different from the body, sense-organs and cognition, yet it is the agent in perception and remembrance.

Autpattika Inborn; originally existent.

Avitatha incorrect.

Bhakti Secondary significative function of words.

Bhāṣya Commentary.

Bhāvanā Efficient force.

Bhāvaśabda Word of activity, becoming.

Bherī Drum.

Brahmacarya Life of a student who is introduced into the Veda. Chastity and purity are required during this training.

Brāhmaṇa One part of the Veda, the other is constituted by *mantras*; guide book for the performance of sacrificial rites.

Buddhi Cognition.

Caitanya Consciousness.

Catvāri four.

Codanā Vedic injunction; it forms the primordially authoritative section of the Vedas, as it is pure *śabda* as *pramāṇa*, i.e., it has no extraneous source leading to error.

Dadhi Thick sour milk.

Darśana Showing, indicating; the main function of *śabda*, language and hermeneutics.

Devatā Deity; there is no concrete information about it available, but its presence is really given through *śabda.*

Dharma "According to the context the assemblage of the Vedic rites prescribed in order to reach 'heaven' after death and welfare in this world or the conduct that is considered to be meritorious because it is recommended by the orthodox tradition and it assures good rebirths" (BIARDEAU, M.) The correct knowledge of it is the aim of Pūrva Mīmāṃsā.

Dravya Substance; offering material.

Dṛṣṭa Visible: whatever can be perceived empirically and named/expressed.

Gauṇa Secondary significative function of words.

Gāvī Corrupted form of *go* (cow).

Go (*gauḥ*) cow.

Goṇī corrupted form of *go*.

Gopotalikā corrupted form of *go*.

Guṇa Quality; what is secondary.

Hasta Hand.

Havirbhāk Recipient of offering (i.e., *devatā*).

Havis Offering.

Homa Pouring libations into fire or water.

Hotṛ Priest.

Icchā Wish, desire, 'urge',

Indriyaviṣaya Pertaining to an object of sense perception.

Iṣṭi Class of sacrifices which consist of offering of milk, butter, rice, barley and other grains.

Itihāsa History; story, the epic. Śabara seems to include *itihāsa* under the category of *smṛti*.

Jāti Class.

Jaghana Hips and loins, hindmost.

Jaghanya Secondary significative function of words.

Jijñāsā Desiderative of the root *jñā*; the desire to know; hermeneutics.

jñā To know, to become acquainted with, understand.

jñāna Knowledge.

Jvalana Fire.

Jyotis Light.

Kāla Time; name of a deity.

Kara Hand.
°*Kāra* Letter (*ga*=*gakāra*).
Karman Ritual act as prescribed in the Veda; action.
Karmaśabda Verb of action.
Kṣaya Destruction.
Kūṭasthanitya Unchangeably eternal.
Lakṣaṇā Expression of secondary meaning.
Mālā Garland.
Māṇavaka Boy, fellow.
Mantra Hymn; formula to be recited in the performance of a sacrificial act. *Mantras* constitute one part of the Veda, the other is *Brāhmaṇas*.
Māsa Month; name of a deity.
Mīmāṃsā Discussion of doubtful points whether in ritual or in philosophy. The investigations into the authority and interpretations of the Veda became two of the classical systems of Indian philosophy. The *Pūrva* (preliminary) *Mīmāṃsā*, i.e. *Mīmāṃsā* prope r, pays special attention to ritual knowledge. Its aim is the correct knowledge of *dharma*. The *Uttara* (final) *Mīmāṃsā* deals mainly with spiritual (not ritual oriented) knowledge of the Vedas and is known as *Vedānta*.
Mleccha Foreigner; The exact significance and meaning of certain words—used even in the Vedas—is only available among *Mlecchas*.
Mukha Face.
Mukhya Primary significative function of words.
Nāda Resonance, which is a conglomeration of various parts and has only an instantaneous existence.
Nāmadheya (Proper) name.
Nimitta Sign; reason.
Niravayava Without parts.
Niṣedha Negative command.
Nitya 'Proper to itself', 'personal', equivalent to *sva*; permanent (in its use), invariable, consistent.
Nityatva Permanence, consistency, invariability.

Nyāya Principle of interpretation, (*Mīmāṃsā*) maxim; one of the six classical systems of Indian philosophy.

Pada Word.

Pāṇi Hand.

Phala Fruit (of sacrifice), result.

Pralaya Destruction.

Pramāṇa Method of knowing and the test of its validity. Six *pramāṇas* are accepted by Śabara.

Pratiṣedha Negative command.

Pratyakṣa Visual perception; sense perception; a *pramāṇa*; cognition in a Vedic statement (Śā. *Bhā*. 1. 1. 2).

Pratyaya Cognition (sometimes identical with *jñāna*).

Purāṇa 'Old book', tale containing mythical matters. Śabara seems to include the *Purāṇas* under the category of *smṛti*.

Pūrva Previous, former, prior to, preliminary.

Rūpa Form, shape.

Śabda Sound, noise, word, speech: *śabda* is *autpattika, apauruṣeya, nitya, aikarūpya, niravayava*. *Śabda* as signifying unit is coexistent with its object. It presents (not re-presents) the object. *Śabda* speaks, makes known something in an authentic authoritative way and is a *pramāṇa*.

Sādhu correct, proper.

Sādhuśabda Correct word; correct set of phonemes as a signifying unit.

Sādhya To be realised.

Sādṛśya Similarity.

Śakti Power, energy.

Śālā House, Hall (for the sacrifice).

Sāmānya Common feature; form of object common to other objects.

Samavāya Inherence.

Saṃbandha Connection, relation (especially between *śabda* and *artha*).

Saṃjñā Name.

Saṃvatsara Year; name of a deity.

Satyam Truth; It emerges as the essence of the pure relationship of *śabda* and *artha*. Language and reality as a whole are *satyam*.

Siddha Established, accomplished, realised.

Siddhi Power.

Śṛṅga Horn.

Śṛṣṭi Creation.

Śruti That which is heard; Vedic revelation; direct statement in the Veda itself or the whole body of the Veda.

Smṛti Remembrance; tradition; It is authoritative, insofar as it is based on the Veda which can only be understood in all its bearing with the help of the *smṛti*.

Soma Sacrificial plant; juice of this plant (drink of immortality).

Sūktabhāk The one to whom hymns are offered (i.e., *devatā*).

Sūrya Sun; name of a deity.

Sūtra Aphoristic text that usually requires commentary or explanation.

Sva one's own; one's natural feature.

Svabhāva own way of being: inherent nature.

Svarga Heaven; Happiness which has no equal in man's experience, i.e., invisible. It results from the sacrifice and is due to the realisation of *dharma*. It is only realised after death by the *ātman*.

Svayam all by itself, by its very nature, of its own accord

Svayaṃpratyaya Cognition out of itself, by its very nature i.e. for Śabara there is knowledge that is valid independently by itself, both in respect of its generation and cognition. It itself certifies its truth.

Upadeśa Pointing out to; instruction; advice.

Upamāna Comparison; a *pramāṇa*.

Utpatti Arising; birth, production, origin.

Vaiśeṣika One of the six classical systems of Indian philosophy.

Vāk Speech.

Vākya Proposition; sentence.

Vākyārtha Object and meaning of a sentence.

Varṇa Phoneme.

Vāyu Wind, air.

Veda Knowledge; the whole body of Sacred Scriptures which entails the *pramāṇa* characteristics in all its parts, and being *apauruṣeya*, it distinguishes itself from all non-Vedic texts.

Vedānta End of the Veda as final conclusion of Vedic teaching; One of the six classical systems of Indian philosophy.

Vedavacana Vedic statement.

Vidhi Vedic injunction which (strictly speaking) alone is the valid source of the knowledge of *dharma;* one type of the ten types of *Brāhmaṇa.*

Vidyā Knowledge.

Vinaṣṭa Perished.

Viśeṣa Particular feature, specific distinction (opposed to *sāmānya*).

Viśeṣaṇa Distinguishing, qualifying factor; specific characteristic which conforms with *ākṛti.*

Viśeṣa What can be distinguished.

Viśiṣṭa Distinguished (object)

Vivarta Emanation, apparent change or transformation.

Vṛṣabha Bull.

Vṛtti Secondary significative function of words.

Vyavahāranitya Permanent (in its usage).

Vyakti Individual.

Vyāmoha Confusion.

BIBLIOGRAPHY

(a) *Primary Sources*

Mīmāṃsādarśana, containing the *Mīmāṃsāsūtra* of Jaimini the *Śābarabhāṣya*, the *Tantravārttika*, and the *Ṭupṭīkā* of Kumārila Bhaṭṭa, *Ānandāśrama Sanskrit Series* 97, Vol. I, [4]1976, Vol. II, [2]1970, Vol. III, [2]1971, Vol. IV, [2]1972, Vol. V, [2]1973, Vol VI, [2]1974, Vol. VII, [2]1974. Poona.

Mīmāṃsāsūtrabhāṣyam I, I, 1-5, Śabarasvāmī's Bhāṣyam zu den Mīṃāmsāsūtren I, 1, 1-5, edited and translated into German by Erich Frauwallner, in : Materialien zur ältesten Erkenntnislehre der Karmamīmāṃsā. (Oest. Akad. der Wiss. Phil-Hist. Kl. Sitzungsberichte 259. Band, 2. Abhandlung) Wien 1968, 7-61.

Ṛgveda Saṃhitā together with the commentary of *Sāyaṇācārya*. Published by Vaidika Saṃśodhana Maṇḍala, Poona.

Ślokavārttika of Śrī Kumārila Bhaṭṭa, with the commentary *Nyāyaratnākara* of Śrī Pārthasārathi Miśra edited and revised by Swāmī Dwākikādāsa Śāstrī, Tara Publications, Varanasi, 1978.

Vākyapadīya of Bhartṛhari with the commentaries *Vṛtti* and *Paddhati* of Vṛṣabhadeva Kāṇḍa I, edited by K.A. Subramania Iyer. (Deccan College Monograph Series, 32. Poona, 1966.)

(*b*) *Secondary Literature*

BHATT, G.P., —Epistemology of the Bhāṭṭa School of Pūrva Mīmāṃsā, Varanasi, 1962.

BIARDEAU, M., —Theorie de la Connaissance et Philosophie de la Parole dans le brahmanisme classique, Paris, 1964.

CHETHIMATTAM, J.B.,—Scriptural Hermeneutics according to the Vedantic Bhasyakaras, in :AMALORPAVADASS,

D.S., (ed.), Research Seminar on Non-Biblical Scriptures, Bangalore, 1974, 360-365.

CHINTAMANI, T.R.,—A Short History of Pūrvamīmāṃsā Literature. Ph. D. thesis, University of Madras.

DATTA, D.M.,—The Six Ways of Knowing. A Critical Study of the Advaita Theory of Knowledge, Calcutta,[2]1972.

DEVASTHALI, G.V.,— On the probable date of Śabarasvāmin, in : Silver Jubilee Volume, Bhandarkar Institute 1917-42, Poona.

DRAVID, R.R.,—Language, Thought and Reality, in : R.C. PANDEYA, S.R. BHATT (eds.)., Knowledge, Culture and Value, Delhi, 1976, 447-453.

D'SA, F.X.,—Kumārila's Theorie der Worterkenntnis. Dissertation. Wien, 1973.

—Revelation without a God. Kumarila's theory of sabdapramanam, in : AMALORPAVADASS, D.S. (ed.), Research Seminar on Non-Biblical Scriptures, Bangalore, 1974, 469-487.

FRAUWALLNER, E., — Das Eindringen der Sprachtheorie in die Indischen philosophischen Systeme. Indologentagung 1959. Verhandluŋgen der Indol. Arbeitstagung in Essen-Bredeny, Göttingen 1960, 239-243.

—Sprachtheorie und Philosophie im Mahābhāṣyam des Patañjali, in : Wienerzeitschrift für die Kunde Süd— und Ostasiens und Archiv für Indische Philosophie 4 (1960) 92-118.

—Mīmāṃsāsūtram I, 1, 6-23, in : Wienerzeitschrift für die Kunde Süd—und Ostasiens und Archiv für Indische Philosophie, 5(1961) 113-124.

—Materialien zur ältesten Erkenntnislehre der Karmamīmāṃsā. (Oest. Akad. der Wiss. Phil. Hist. Kl. Sitzungsberichte 259. Band, 2. Abhandlung) Wien. 1968.

GADAMER, H.G.,—Wahrheit und Methode. Grundzüge einer philosophischen Hermeneutik, Tübingen 2nd ed. 1965.

GARGE, D.V.,—The Contribution of the Śābara-Bhāṣya to Ṛgveda Exegesis; or the Treatment by Śabara of the Ṛgveda-Passages cited in his Bhāṣya, in; Bulletin of the

Deccan College Post-Graduate and Research Institute, Poona, 3.4.pp.531-546.

—Citations in Śābara-Bhāṣya, Deccan College Dissertation Series 8, Poona, 1952.

GREGORIOS, P.—Hermeneutics in India today in the Light of the World Debate, in : The Indian Journal of Theology, 28 (1979) 1-14.

IYER, K.A.S..—Bhartṛhari on vyākaraṇa as a means of attaining mokṣa, iṅ : The Adyar Library Bulletin 27, Parts 1-2,Mag. 1964, pp. 112-131.

—Bhartṛhari, A study of the Vākyapadīya in the light of the Ancient Commentaries, Poona, 1969.

JHA, G., —Śābara-Bhāṣya (English Translation in 3 Volumes) : Gaekwad's Oriental Series, No. 66, 70, 73, Baroda, 1933.

—Pūrva Mīmāṃsā in its Sources, Varanasi, 1964.

KANE, P.V.,—History of Dharmaśāstra. Government Oriental Series Class B, No. 6. Second Edition Vol. I-V Part I, [2]1968-75; Vol, V Part II, 1962, Poona.

KUPPUSWAMI, B.,—A Modern Review of Hindu Dharma, in : Journal of Dharma, 1 (1975) 118-130.

LADRIERE, J.,—The Performativity of Liturgical Language, in : Concilium 2 (1973) No.9, 50-62.

LEHMANN, K.,—Hermeneutics, in : RAHNER, K., ERNST, C., SMYTH, K., (eds.), Sacramentum Mundi. An Encyclopedia of Theology. 6 Vol., Vol. III. Banglore 1975, 23-27.

LIENHARD, S.,—Einige Bemerkungen über Śabdabrahman and vivarta bei Bhavabhūti,in : Wienerzeitschrift für die Kunde Süd-und Ostasiens und Archiv für Indische Philosophie, 12 (1968) 216-219.

MANICKAM, T.M.,—Manu's Vision on the Hindu Dharma, in : Journal of Dharma 1 (1975) 101-117.

MISRA, R.S.,—Studies in Philosophy and Religion, Varanasi, 1971.

MISRA, U.,—Index to the English Translation of Shabara-Bhāṣya (Published as Numbers 66, 70 and 73 in the Gaekwad's Oriental Series), Gaekwad's Oriental Series No. 103, Baroda, 1945.

—Critical Bibilography of Mīmāṃsā, in : JHA, G., Pūrva-Mīmāṃsā in its Sources, (Appendix), Varanasi ²1964.

MURTI, T.R.V.,—The Central Philosophy of Buddhism, A Study of the Mādhyamika System. London, ⁴1974.

—Some Thoughts on the Indian Philosophy of Language. Presidential Address on the Indian Philosophical Congress, 37th Session (Chandigarh) 1963.

—Some Comments on the Philosophy of Language in the Indian Context, in : Journal of Indian Philosophy (Toronto) 2 (1974) 321-331.

—Knowledge and Truth, in : R. C. PANDEYA, S.R. BHATT (eds.), Knowledge, Culture and Value, Delhi, 1976. (Motilal Banarsidass)

MURTY,K.S.,—Revelation and Reason in Advaita Vedānta, Delhi, ²1974. (Motilal Banarsidass)

PANDEY, S.L.,—Indian Views of Theological Statements, in : Bharata Manisha Quarterly, 1 (1976), No. 4, 33-41.

PANDEYA, R.C..—The Problem of Meaning in Indian Philosophy, Delhi, 1963. (Motilal Banarsidass)

PANIKKAR., R.,—Die Begründung des hermeneutischen Pluralismus im Hinduismus, in; Kerygma und Mythos VI, Bd. II Entmythologisierung und Bild., Hamburg 1964, 119-136.

—The Vedic Experience. Mantramañjarī. An Anthology of the Vedas for Modern Man and Contemporary Celebration, London, 1977.

PATHAK, C., – Brahma-Jijñāsā as a Fundamental Hermeneutics, in:Bharata Manisha Quarterly 1 (1976) No. 4,13-27.

RAJA, K.K.,—Indian Theories of Meaning, Madras, 1963.

RAMAN, N.S.S.,—The Problem of Philosophical Translation (with special reference to the idealist texts of Indian and Western Philosophy), in : Indian Philosophical Annual, 7 (1971) 1-16.

—The Language of Myth in Religion, in : Journal of Dharma 2 (1977) 372-381.

RUEGG, D.S., –Contributions à l' histoire de la philosophie linguistique indienne, Paris, 1959.

SASTRI, G.,—The Philosophy of Word and Meaning, Calcutta, 1959.

WILSON, H.H.,—Rig Veda. Translations and Notes. Vol. III, Poona 1926.

ZANGENBERG, F.,—Śabaraḥ und seine philosophischen Quellen, in : Wienerzeitschrift für die Kunde Süd- und Ostasiens und Archiv für Indische Philosophie, 6 (1962) 60-77.

INDEX